KT-546-842

THIS BOOK BELONGS TO
ACS WOODLEE
LONDON, SURREY
WITHDRAWN

WITHDRAWN

CHINA
THE DRAGON AWAKES

DISCOVERING our HERITAGE

By Tony Zurlo

THIS BOOK BELONGS TO
ACS WOODLEE
LONDON ROAD (A30)
EGHAM, SURREY
TW20 0HS

DILLON PRESS
New York

Maxwell Macmillan Canada
Toronto

Maxwell Macmillan International
New York   Oxford   Singapore   Sydney

Credits and Acknowledgments

In China, dozens of people deserve credit for their warm friendship, especially my students at Hebei Teachers' University, most of whom are now graduate students or teachers throughout China. Among those who deserve my special thanks for making me feel part of an extended family are Li Yi, Cao Bo, Xin Ji Hong, Zhang Yan Lian, Zhu Xiu Ling, and Wu Guoqi.

I want to thank my former department head at Hebei Teachers' University, Dong Qiming, and my colleagues Mao Zhuo Liang and Wang Xin Li for their patience and understanding.

There are two people who have tirelessly interpreted, explained, and reexplained China to me: Gu Linli and Lu Wei. Lu Wei, who spent many hours helping me with pronunciation of words and understanding subtle but important differences in Chinese culture, also wrote all of the Chinese characters in the book.

A hundred more names should be mentioned, but I would need the pages taken up by the contents of this book, so I'll just say to my Chinese friends, *"Wo ai nimen."* "I love you" for opening your hearts to me and for making me feel more Chinese than American.

Photo Credits

Cover: Tony Zurlo.
Nanjing Slides/Chinese Consulate, Houston: 60-61. William Thomas: 11, 25, 27, 29, 31, 37, 67, 94, 95, 100. Tony Zurlo: 9, 12, 19, 33, 35, 45, 51, 65, 74, 76, 79, 85, 98, 104, 107, 111.

Library of Congress Cataloging-in-Publication Data

Zurlo, Tony
    China : the dragon awakes / by Tony Zurlo.
       p. cm. — (Discovering our heritage)
    Includes bibliographical references and index.
    ISBN 0-87518-596-7
    1. China—Civilization—Juvenile literature. [1. China.] I. Title. II. Series.
DS721.Z87 1994
951—dc20   94-8015

Describes the geography, history, folklore, family life, education, sports and recreation, and culture of China, including a chapter about Chinese Americans.

Copyright © 1994 by Tony Zurlo

All rights reserved. No part of this book may be reproduced or transmitted in any form or by any means, electronic or mechanical, including photocopying, recording, or by any information storage and retrieval system, without permission in writing from the Publisher.

Dillon Press
Macmillan Publishing Company
866 Third Avenue
New York, NY 10022

Maxwell Macmillan Canada, Inc.
1200 Eglinton Avenue East
Suite 200
Don Mills, Ontario M3C 3N1

Macmillan Publishing Company is part of the Maxwell Communication Group of Companies.

First edition

Printed in the United States of America

10 9 8 7 6 5 4 3 2

Contents

Fast Facts about China

Official Name: *People's Republic of China*. In Chinese, Zhongguo, or "Middle Kingdom."

Capital: Beijing. In Chinese, "North Capital."

Location: East Asia, south of Russia and north of Southeast Asia. To the east lie Japan and North and South Korea. India, Pakistan, and Afghanistan are on China's western borders.

Area: 3,696,100 square miles (9,572,900 square kilometers). **Greatest distances:** northeast to southeast, 3,418 miles (5,500 kilometers); northeast to west, 3,231 miles (5,200 kilometers).

Elevation: *Highest*—Mount Everest in Tibet (borders Nepal), 29,028 feet (8,848 meters) above sea level. *Lowest*—Turpan (Turfan) Depression, 426 feet (130 meters) below sea level, in Xinjiang Republic.

Population: 1.2 billion (1990 census). *Distribution*—80 percent rural; 20 percent urban. *Density*—varies greatly, but in the south it is as high as 1,500 persons per square mile (580 per square kilometer).

Form of Government: Republic, with power centered in the National People's Congress, controlled by the Communist Party.

Important Products: *Agriculture*—rice, wheat, cotton, maize, fruits, vegetables. *Industry*—coal, iron and steel, oil and gas, textiles, fishing, construction.

Basic Unit of Money: Yuan (approximately 5 1/2 yuan equal 1 U.S. dollar).

Major Languages: Mandarin Chinese, English, Russian.

Major Religions: Officially, religions are discouraged, although they are not forbidden. Islam, Christianity, Buddhism, and Daoism are the most popular, with millions of followers each.

Flag: Red with a gold star in the upper left, flanked by four small gold stars.

National Anthem: "March of the Volunteers."

Major Holidays: Spring Festival (Chinese New Year)—varies with the lunar calendar, but it begins in late January or early February and lasts for 15 days. National Day—October 1.

1. Unusual Landscapes

Towering mountains, vast deserts, and the Pacific Ocean provide China with natural barriers against invasion. Within China, nature has sometimes purred like a kitten, allowing for great harvests. Often, however, nature has roared like an angry lion, destroying lives and homes with floods and earthquakes.

For over 3,000 years the Chinese viewed their land as almost sacred. Spectacular mountains in the southwest soar 20,000 feet (6,100 meters) into the clouds, like rocky stairs to the heavens. In the northwest the snow-covered mountains are called Tian Shan (Tee-ēn shāan), or Celestial Mountains. (See Appendix One, page 114, for an explanation of the pronunciation of Chinese words.) Rivers cutting through mountains have left mysterious peaks floating above the mist.

China's land area ranks third in the world. But deserts and mountains make up over two-thirds of the country. Many other parts are too dry or rocky to farm. As a result, less than 11 percent of the land can be used for farming.

China shares borders with many countries: Russia and Mongolia to the north; Vietnam, Laos, Myanmar, India, Bhutan, and Nepal in the south; India, Pakistan, Kazakhstan, Kyrgyzstan, Tajikistan, and Afghanistan in the west. To the east are North Korea, the Yellow Sea, East China Sea, and South China Sea. South Korea, Japan, Taiwan, and the Philippines all lie within 600 miles (970 kilometers) of China's 8,700-mile-long (14,000-kilometer) coastline.

Northern China

Northern China extends northward from the Huanghe (Hwáang-húh—Yellow River) and includes the large region north of Korea called Manchuria. Beijing (Bǎy-jīng), China's capital and second largest city, with ten million people, sits in the northern tip of the North China Plain. Together, the North China Plain and Shandong (Shān-dōng) Peninsula are the size of Texas, but the area has more people than the entire United States.

More than 400 million people live along the 3,000-mile-long (4,828-kilometer) Huanghe. On its journey to the sea, the Huanghe deposits a rich yellow soil (loess) along its banks. During their four- to eight-month growing season, farmers raise crops such as wheat, maize, barley, soybeans, peanuts, cotton, and fruits.

The Huanghe has also earned the nickname the "River of Sorrow." Often in history, the river has raged over its banks, washing away whole villages. In 1959, floods killed nearly two million people in northern China. Today, dams and canals help control floods.

Winters on the North China Plain are cold, dry, and dusty. In the summer, moisture blows in from the ocean, keeping the area hot with highs in the 90°s F (30°s C), and humid. Most of Beijing's 20 to 30 inches (51 to 77 centimeters) of annual rain falls in the summer.

Manchuria meets Russia's Siberia in the frigid northeastern corner of China. The three provinces there are heavily populated despite the cold climate. Winter temperatures of -20°F (-29°C) and lower are common well into March. People in Harbin, the capital of Heilongjiang (Hāy-lóng-gē-aang) Province, cut blocks of ice from the river and build huge ice palaces, land-

Mountains north of the Great Wall and Beijing

scapes, and other figures for display. Rich in minerals, especially coal, this part of China has large industries. In the summer, several rivers supply plenty of water for farming. But the growing season is short.

Southern China

The Qin Ling (Chín lǐng) Mountains in central China provide a natural boundary between northern and southern China. There are several ranges that branch north and south of the Qin Ling Mountains as well. In fact, much of China's seacoast is mountainous.

The other major river in China is the Changjiang (Cháng-gee-āang—Yangtze River). About 3,100 miles (4,989 kilometers) long, it is the world's third longest river. For 700 miles (1,130 kilometers) inland, it is deep enough for cargo ships to sail. Smaller boats can travel upriver over 1,000 miles (1,600 kilometers) into Sichuan (Sìh-chwaān) Province. Nearly 400 million people live along the Changjiang basin.

Like the Huanghe, the Changjiang adds rich minerals to the land along its path. Floods, however, continue to leave behind death and destruction. In 1991, after weeks of heavy rains, the Changjiang flooded for hundreds of miles. More than a thousand people died and hundreds of thousands lost their homes.

At Shanghai (Shàng-hǎi) on the East China Sea, the Changjiang fans out into a wide, fertile delta, a system of low-lands and canals that supports 30 million people. The water is used for almost everything, from transportation and fishing to washing clothes.

Shanghai marks the coastal midpoint between northern and southern China. China's largest city at 12 million people, Shanghai has been an international seaport for hundreds of years. It is also an important educational and industrial center.

Southern China gets rain year-round. Hong Kong, which will become a part of China in 1997, averages over 80 inches (205 centimeters) a year. The heaviest rains come in the summer, though, when monsoons (storms from the ocean) and typhoons (hurricanes) pound the continent.

In the far south, China is subtropical. Hainan Island, located directly east of Vietnam, is hot and humid most of the time. And to the west, in the mountains bordering Myanmar, the temperature is always above freezing.

In the south, the Chinese are close to hills or mountains. Farmers terrace the hills and irrigate them with pumps. They grow crops there all year, which yield up to three harvests. Rice is their major crop, but other important crops include sugarcane,

Pavilion, rock, and lotus blossoms at West Lake, Hangshou ▶

silk, tobacco, and tea.

In southwestern China, the land turns into lush mountain forests. Near Sichuan's capital, Chengdu (Chúng-dū), bamboo forests provide a natural home for the giant panda. In southeastern Sichuan, the Sichuan Basin supports about 70 million people. Because of the rich soil and mild, wet climate there, the farmers have become among China's most productive.

Scenic Spots in the South

The Chinese are proud of their country's scenery. Marco Polo, the 13th-century Italian explorer who lived for many years in China, described Hangzhou (Háang-joē) as "the noblest and most beautiful city on earth." Nearby is an island named Three Ponds Reflecting the Moon, with lotus ponds and small lakes

filled with goldfish. Another city famous for its lovely scenery is Fuzhou (Fú-joē) across from the island of Taiwan. The Chinese call Fuzhou, crowded with gardens, "Paradise on Earth."

The area around the city of Guilin (Gwày-lín) is famous all over the world from Chinese paintings. East and west of the city, bamboo forests and small fishing villages line the Li River. Fishermen there are famous for the cormorants they train to catch fish with their beaks. Halos of fog crown the

Yangso, near Guilin, in southern China

cone-shaped mountains that sit along the river. A poet once compared these mountains to jade needles, and the twisting river to a
ribbon of blue silk.

Outer China

Western and northwestern China contrast sharply with the rest of
the country. Made up mostly of deserts and some of the highest
mountains in the world, the area includes Xinjiang (Shīn-geē-
aang), Inner Mongolia (Nei Monggol), and Tibet (Xizang).

Xinjiang's salt lakes and deserts are bordered in the north
by 20,000-foot-high (6,100-meter) mountains. The entire area
gets about 10 inches (25 to 80 centimeters) of rain a year. So
most people herd animals, work at handicrafts, or run small
businesses.

Inner Mongolia is dominated by the Gobi Desert. It forms
an impressive barrier to land transportation for thousands of
miles. People have established towns along isolated rivers and
valleys.

South of Xinjiang and Inner Mongolia, the land changes to
grassy plains, 12,000 feet (3,700 meters) above sea level. Here in
Tibet are the foothills of the world's highest mountain chain, the
Himalayas. Tibet, nicknamed the Rooftop of the World, shares
the world's highest mountain peak, Mount Everest (29,028 feet,
or 8,848 meters), with Nepal.

Economic Growth

China's economic progress in recent years has outpaced all of
the industrialized nations'. The coastal provinces have grown the

fastest. Over half of China's wealth comes from the seven coastal provinces and the three self-governing cities of Beijing, Shanghai, and Tianjin (Teē-en giñ).

Business and farming in Guangdong Province, in the southeast, are flourishing. Guangzhou (Gwǎang-joē), known as Canton to foreigners, has long been a major port. The surrounding area includes several Special Economic Zones (SEZs) established by the government in the 1980s to encourage foreigners to set up businesses in China.

In southwestern China, Chengdu street vendors sell everything from vegetables to life insurance. In a country where the average family makes between $300 and $500 a year, a few have become extremely rich. One Sichuan farmer made over $4,000 in a recent year selling potted plants.

In northern China, the villagers of Daqiuzhuang (Dà-chēeu-chuāng), about 100 miles (160 kilometers) southeast of Beijing, claim to make over $8,000 a year. But the most prosperous part of China will be the island of Hong Kong. With 5.5 million people, it is the third leading financial center in the world. In 1997, the island will switch from British to Chinese rule, but will be allowed to keep its capitalist economy and local government.

Governing One-fifth of the World's People

Governing the world's most populous country is a difficult task. China is divided into 22 provinces, 5 self-governing regions, and 3 self-governing cities. Provinces consist of counties and the larger cities, while counties are made up of townships and villages.

In villages, people vote for members of their local and

county governments. Then those elected officials select representatives to the provincial government. When the provincial government meets, it chooses officials to the National People's Congress (NPC). The 3,000 members of the NPC, including representatives from Hong Kong, Macao, Taiwan, and "Overseas" Chinese groups, meet yearly in Beijing to pass laws.

When Mao Zedong (Máo Dzéh-dōng, 1893–1976) led the Chinese peasants to military victory in 1949, he made sure the new constitution put the Communist Party in control of the country. Under Mao, the Chinese developed pride as an independent, unified nation.

Under his rule, China struggled to build an economic foundation. But political turmoil discouraged progress. Shortly after Mao's death in 1976, Deng Xiaoping (Dèng Seē-ŏw-píng) became party leader. Now retired, Deng brought peace and order back to the country. Today, the most important leaders are Prime Minister Li Peng, Deputy Premier Zhu Rongyi, and Communist Party General Secretary Jiang Zemin.

The Communist Party

Anyone can run for office in China, but it helps to be a member of the Chinese Communist Party (CCP). In 1991, 66 percent of the members of the National People's Congress were members of the Chinese Communist Party. Every five years, the party (about 51 million members) selects delegates to meet in Beijing. Over 2,000 delegates attended the 14th Party Congress in October 1992. The party's Central Committee, numbering more than 200, determines the policies for the Communist Party.

The Central Committee elects 20 members to sit on the

party's Politburo (Political Bureau). Then seven members of the Politburo are named to the Standing Committee. The real power in China resides with the Standing Committee. Its members determine policies and submit them to the NPC for approval. At this highest level of power, the final decisions are usually made by a single leader, who can remove those opposed to his policies.

Essentially, China is a dictatorship. The people have no direct ability to influence the government. Sometimes the most powerful person in China is not a government official. For example, Deng Xiaoping has not held any official position for many years. But even though his health has declined rapidly in the 1990s, his ideas are still followed.

The Future

Since the late 1970s, young Chinese have expressed their desire for more democracy. They also complain that their leaders are too old—several are in their eighties—to lead China into the 21st century. Open opposition to their rule could return the country to widespread civil unrest and even civil war.

Mass demonstrations spread throughout China in the spring of 1989. While people around the world watched on television, the government sent armed troops to break up the unrest. Throughout Beijing, troops fired into crowds of demonstrators. And at Tiananmen (Teē-en-ān-mún) Square, in downtown Beijing, tanks crushed a replica of the Statue of Liberty built by university students as a symbol of their demand for democracy. In the capital city alone, thousands were killed or injured. Nations around the world protested to China's leaders.

2. The People

One out of every five persons in the world lives in China. With 1.2 billion people, China is the world's largest nation. About 400 million live in cities. Twice that many, 800 million, live in rural areas, most of them poor farmers, or peasants.

Unlike Americans, who come from all the nationalities of the world, 94 percent of the Chinese claim common ancestors: the Han (Hàhn). The Han people, living near Xi'an (Syēe-āan) in central China, became China's second dynasty, or ruling family. The Han ruled China from 206 B.C. to A.D. 220.

About 6 percent of the Chinese (72 million people) belong to one of the 55 official minority groups. Numbering over 13 million, the Zhuang in Guangxi Autonomous Region make up the largest minority. Other important minority groups include the Hui, Uighur, Yi, Miao, Manchu, Tibetan, and Mongol.

Kingdom of Bicycles

China has been called a Kingdom of Bicycles. The Chinese own more bicycles, 365 million, than the United States has people. In the cities, special bicycle lanes are built on each side of major roads. During morning and afternoon rush hours, thousands of bike riders pack these lanes.

In the country, men and women ride bicycles to their farms, often a few miles outside the villages. They carry everything on their bikes, from babies to furniture. Many farmers carry crops by bike to sell at city markets.

In cities, people often ride buses wherever they go. Buses cost only a few pennies to ride. However, the buses are so crowded that sometimes it is impossible to get on one. In Beijing, a modern subway carries hundreds of thousands of people daily to work, schools, and recreational areas.

A Proud People

The Chinese call their country Zhongguo (Zhōng-gwáw), or the Middle Kingdom. They called it "middle" to indicate that China was the center of the world. The Chinese believed that outside their kingdom there lived only uncivilized people, or barbarians. To their credit, until the 18th century, the Chinese had achieved more than most other countries. They invented printing, the compass, and gunpowder. And they were far ahead of Europe in knowledge of irrigation, astronomy, medicine, and ceramics.

A common written language is another source of pride to the Chinese. It takes a long time to memorize the characters. For example, to read a daily newspaper, a person has to know about 4,000 characters. Officials estimate that close to 75 percent of the Chinese people can read and write.

Great inventions, a common written language, and a long, unified history have helped make the Chinese a proud people. But the glue that has held the society together is the family.

Through the centuries, the Chinese have stressed the importance of family loyalty. They have a saying: "Falling leaves settle on their roots." Even family members who travel or work elsewhere returned to their homeland whenever possible.

People board a crowded bus in Beijing.

The Family and Confucianism

In the 6th century B.C., a famous Chinese philosopher named Confucius (Kong FuZi—Kŏong Fōo-dz) taught men how to govern wisely. Not all his ideas were original; he based his teachings on the traditions and customs of the early Chinese kingdoms.

The basis of all social order, according to Confucius, is the family living in harmony. The father should lead by always being kind and balanced in his behavior. Only those who were model fathers and husbands could be good rulers. Leaders of the community should behave as model fathers, setting a good example. If they did, people would obey willingly.

Confucius said that wisdom comes only with age. He also believed that only men should be leaders. Therefore, the oldest male was the family head. If he led by good behavior, then his family would follow his example. If each family acted properly, then their village would run smoothly. And peaceful villages contributed to a prosperous nation.

Each family member had to obey strict rules. These rules

put women in an inferior position. Men had total control over women's lives. For example, men thought tiny feet on women were a mark of beauty. So between the ages of about 4 and 13, girls had to live with their feet bound. In old China, they learned the "home" skills of sewing, cooking, and cleaning. And the majority of women worked in the fields. Only men learned the art of governing, so women were not formally educated.

Confucius also taught that family members should accept responsibility for one another's actions. Everybody felt the pressure to behave well. Because people who acted foolishly embarrassed the whole family, everyone would "lose face." The individual had to think of the group welfare before acting.

Besides not allowing women equality, Confucianism had another major weakness. It emphasized learning by memorizing, not by questioning and thinking. This was a major reason that China lagged behind Europe in scientific discoveries by the 18th century.

Traditional Myths and Religions

The Chinese believe deeply that life should be enjoyed. At the center of their social values is the principle that people should treat one another with kindness. These principles were learned from Confucianism, not organized religion. Confucius told his disciples, "You are not yet able to serve men; how can you serve spirits?"

Even with this emphasis on this world's life, the Chinese have also believed in spirits and gods. The common story about the creation says that in the beginning there was a huge egg, and in this egg was darkness and chaos. One day, the ancestor of the Chinese, Pangu, was born inside the egg. He was disturbed by the darkness, so he began hitting at the inside of the egg with an axe until the shell broke. The light part of the egg rose up and became the sky. The yolk spread out to become the earth.

Afraid that the sky and earth would come together again, Pangu stood up so that his head held up the sky and his feet steadied the earth. As Pangu grew taller, he pushed the sky up further. But the effort of keeping the sky and earth apart exhausted him so much that eventually he fell down, dying.

Then a miraculous event occurred. Pangu's breath changed into the wind and clouds. His voice became the thunder. His eyes turned into the sun and the moon, while his body changed into mountains, his blood into rivers. His hair and skin became flowers and grass. Pangu's teeth and bones became the metals, rocks, jade, and other minerals. Thus, in his death, Pangu created the earth.

Another popular story describes the creation of human beings. The goddess Nü Wa wandered the world alone, with only the birds and fishes as company. One day, while sitting next to a pond, she took some mud and began shaping it to look like her reflection in the water. As soon as she put the figure on the ground, it began to move about and call Nü Wa "mama." Nü Wa named this figure Ren (rén), or Human. Happy with her creation, Nü Wa made many more. Because she realized that they must die, Nü Wa began matching male and female so that the world would continue to have humans. In history, Nü Wa has often been honored as the goddess of marriage.

Native Chinese religion is very different from Western religions. The deities the Chinese honored were more personal, with lives in the afterworld much like the lives they had on earth. Usually, the deities were identified with either ancestors or with nature.

For example, in ancient China, the ruling classes believed that they had power and privilege because of their ancestors' success. As a result, the ruling classes would pay tribute to a particular ancestor they considered most influential. They also believed that their ancestors could influence the destiny of family members still alive. So people would offer sacrifices of food and drink to their ancestors. This custom was common throughout China. As a result, each locality had many deities.

Throughout much of Chinese history, the forces of nature controlled the lives of the people. They suffered annually from disasters such as floods, droughts, and famine. Therefore, the people believed that nature itself had supernatural powers. Mountains especially have been considered holy because they seem to rise into the heavens. Tai Shan (Tìe-shāan), in eastern China (Shandong Province), is still considered one of the sacred mountains in China. Temples are built on these mountains, where priests offer services to the various gods.

The religion closely identified with nature in China is Daoism (Dào-ism), which means the "way of life." Its origins are traced to a man who may have lived around the time of Confucius (551–479 B.C.). He was called Lao Zi (Lǎu Dz), which simply means "Old Master." The main doctrine of Daoism teaches people to live naturally, to discard everything that is not part of their own human nature. By realizing that everything in nature inherits its own set of natural rules, each person learns that he or she also has a natural way to behave.

One part of Daoism that was inherited from early Chinese

philosophy was the doctrine of yin-yang (yīn-yáng). This idea proposes that in nature there are always opposing forces that work together to create harmony and balance. One force, yin, is female in nature. It is represented by the earth; it is passive but fertile, soft, mysterious, and secretive. The other force, yang, is male in nature. It is represented by heaven; it is active and direct, and brings light and openness.

Neither yin nor yang is good or bad, because the two exist as a unit. The earth, yin, carries and gives forth life. This feminine force is actually the model for people to follow. Daoism suggests that the ideal person should be passive, like the earth; natural, instead of trying to dominate. Only with yin-like qualities can people receive truth. One of the poems in the Daoist book, *The Way of Life*, teaches that:

> The great land is a place
> To which the streams descend;
> It is the concourse and
> The female of the world:
> Quiescent, underneath,
> It overcomes the male.

From Daoism comes the idea that truth is beyond logic and can only be found by cleaning out our minds of everyday concerns. Only then can the force of yang do its part in people's search for truth. Therefore, yin and yang work together as a unit.

From this origin, Daoism was changed over the centuries from these simple ideas of following one's own nature to a religion full of magic and superstition. A priestly class developed that claimed to know the secret ways to commune with the gods.

Over the centuries, Daoism was mixed with traditional ancestor worship and the third major religious movement to influence Chinese life, Buddhism.

Buddhism reached China in the first century A.D. The Chinese people then entered into a long period of unrest. Peasants were selling land to pay taxes to the rich landowners, making the landowners even richer. The Confucian ideas didn't seem to be working for the masses of people. And Daoism was still more suitable for mystics than for the common people.

The form of Buddhism that became popular in China offered the people many comforts. One was its emphasis on salvation in another world after physical death. This gave the people hope for escape from their miserable living conditions. Another comfort the poor got from Buddhism was its idea that worldly riches are actually obstacles to salvation.

Buddhism also is a tolerant religion. So the Chinese took Buddhist concepts and added them to their own local beliefs about ancestors and nature. The Chinese found nothing in Buddhism that discouraged this. Buddhism is a compassionate religion as well. Chinese Buddhism taught that people who have found the truth while still alive can delay their entry into eternal happiness after they die in order to help save others.

The Chinese Today

Although the Communist government officially allows freedom of religion, the leaders keep a close watch on all religions. The Communists say religions are nothing more than a collection of superstitions that mislead the people.

But an equally important reason for resisting formal reli-

Gold Buddhas at the Jade Buddha Temple in Shanghai

gions is national pride: In China's history, most religions have stood for foreign intervention. Even Buddhism, which came from India, was acceptable to officials only after they molded it to fit in closely with Confucian and Daoist ideas.

The Chinese have also been skeptical of any religion that claimed absolute truth. Typically, they absorb various ideas and then blend them with their own traditional beliefs.

This seems to be happening now under Communism. Confucianism, for example, was criticized severely by the Communists in the 1950s and 1960s, but the Chinese continue to follow many Confucian ideas. The Communists never managed to replace the strong unity of the family with loyalty to the Communist Party. The family has survived as the major social group in the society. Confucian respect for the elderly still prevails as well. During holidays, the elders expect visits from younger relatives. In fact, the Communists actually reinforced this Confucian concept by passing a law that requires children to take care of their parents.

Although most Chinese today would not claim to be Buddhist, many still follow Buddhist burial customs and honor Buddhist holy days. Throughout China, Buddhist temples are being restored and ceremonies are held in public.

The influence of Daoism is still strong, especially in the arts. Most Chinese painting throughout the centuries has concentrated on nature, with human activities blending in with, not dominating, the environment. This idea of being a part of the harmonious whole of creation is the center of Daoist belief.

Mao Zedong tried to elevate Communist philosophy into a kind of religion. But the main effect of Communism has been to stunt economic growth. True to their nature, the Chinese appear to be moving away from Communism for a very practical reason: It has been unsuccessful. In the end, the Chinese, as always, will keep what blends with their traditions and brings prosperity, and will discard that which doesn't work well.

Women: "Half the Sky"

Mao Zedong said that women "held up half the sky," so they should play an equal role with men in building the new world. When the Communists took control, the first reform bill passed by the government was the Marriage Law. For the first time in China's history, women were allowed to own property, both men and women could choose their own spouses, and women were permitted to get a divorce.

Women have made gains in China's society. Now, almost all women work full-time outside the home. They have jobs in

Silk-factory workers sort cocoons.

industry, commerce, and education. They serve in the police, military, and government. In many hospitals, most of the doctors are women.

But tradition is difficult to change. Men still hold most of the high leadership positions. The higher-paying jobs usually go to men. And most students in the secondary schools and colleges are still male. Women graduating from college find it more difficult than men to obtain good jobs.

Guanxi

In modern China, almost everyone has a large network of friends. Besides family, friends come from a person's place of work (*danwei*—Dāan-wày) or school. Some friends can get special favors because they have influence in "high places." People might be able to find good housing, a television, telephone service, or jobs for their children by asking friends for help.

This system of friends-helping-friends is called *guanxi* *(guāan-syee)*. It means "personal connections." The Communists have tried to eliminate this type of exchange of favors. They want everybody to have equal opportunities and treatment. But this kind of mutual help has always been a custom in China, so it will be almost impossible to stop. Besides, the Communist officials themselves use the system of *guanxi* extensively.

Problems and Prospects

The change in the life of the Chinese since the Communists came to power in 1949 is remarkable. So many long-held traditions and customs have been challenged or discarded. But there are problems. The educated people are often unhappy because the government decides what jobs most people are to have. To change jobs, people must first get permission from the Communist Party officials at the place of work. In addition, people are supposed to live wherever assigned by the government.

Adults must carry resident ID cards at all times. When traveling, if asked, they must show the card to authorities. Even to get a room in a hotel, they often have to show a letter of introduction stamped by their *danwei*.

Compared with their grandparents, however, the Chinese live in luxury, especially in the cities. For the first half of the 20th century, millions died yearly from starvation, disease, and abuse. Today, almost everyone in China has plenty of food, shelter, and clothing. Almost all Chinese children attend at least elementary school, even in the rural areas.

Today, the government is opening the economy to free enterprise. Private businesses and shops are common throughout the country. In 1992, the number of self-employed reached more than 22 million. This independence is spreading into the regional governments as well. Sichuan Province, for example, without any money from the central government in Beijing, is building a railroad to the coastal province of Guangdong.

An open market with competitive prices in Dalian

Prior to the 1980s, the government controlled every part of the economy, including jobs. Workers received lifetime assignments, a system called the "iron rice bowl." How well they worked had little impact on their future. Although it is not a common practice, government-owned companies are beginning to dismiss workers who are not productive. Officials in large cities are organizing job fairs for people who want to work for private businesses.

Over a decade of stability under Communist rule has brought rapid economic growth. China's economy is the third largest in the world, according to some experts. From watches to clothes, China's trade with the United States is enormous. In the United States, two out of every five toys and one out of every four Nike athletic shoes sold throughout the country are made in China. China has become the seventh largest trading partner of the United States.

In recent years, living conditions in the cities have improved much faster than those in the countryside. As a result, peasants have protested against too many taxes and local government corruption. Chinese officials take these protests seriously because unrest among peasants has foreshadowed all successful rebellions throughout China's history.

Soon a new generation will lead China. The Chinese don't want to give up their new prosperity, but they realize they must control their economic growth. A proud people, the Chinese will continue working hard to build their country.

3. Oldest Country in the World

China may be the oldest country in the world. At least 5,000 years ago, villagers near Xi'an farmed millet, raised pigs and dogs, hunted with bows, and fished. They also painted and carved clan and ancestry markers on their pottery. Three powerful kingdoms existed along the Huanghe: Xia (Syàh, 2200–1750 B.C.), Shang (Shāng, 1750–1040 B.C.), and Zhou (Joē, 1040–256 B.C.).

China's name, however, comes from the Qin (Chín) dynasty. Qin Shi Huang (Chín Shǐ Huáng— "First Qin Emperor"), ruler of the state of Qin, conquered most of China in 221 B.C. One of his projects put a million men to work connecting old walls and building new ones. Within ten years, the Great Wall, a symbol of Chinese unity ever since, stretched 3,728 miles (6,000 kilometers) across northern China, according to legend.

The Great Wall north of Beijing

Dynastic Rule

One historian writes that China has "the world's longest tradition of autocracy." The country was governed by emperors until 1912, and since then by strong dictators.

The emperor, as the Son of Heaven, had unlimited authority to reward or punish. Intimidation, torture, and death were often used against opponents. A major reason for strict loyalty to the emperor was the very practical purpose of keeping this huge country unified and orderly.

The people looked to the emperor as a father. By his behavior, he was supposed to set an example for others to follow. Under a good ruler, the country stayed calm and the common people prospered. Often the country would be so peaceful that people didn't even lock their doors.

The Social Order

Confucian morality teaches that people who think of themselves first are selfish. Individualism endangers the survival of society. As a result, the Chinese value the group above the individual. The emphasis on group can be seen in the way the Chinese have always governed themselves.

At the local level, opinions are aired within specific groups. Families settle their own differences, the father having the final word. Problems between neighbors or at work are solved by their leaders. If these attempts fail, village elders hear appeals. Today, appeals might go to Communist Party officials at each level.

The goal, after all, is to settle problems within the primary group. The Chinese feel embarrassed and fear they will lose face

A stone statue of Confucius at Qufu ▶

by revealing their problems to outsiders.

Before the 20th century, leaders were men who passed three-day-long examinations on Confucianism. Their duty was to take care of local issues, especially tax collection. The common people also looked to the "nobility" for leadership. These men owned large amounts of land or were successful in business. They distributed supplies and food after natural disasters such as floods and earthquakes. In addition, they directed public works projects such as building roads and dams.

The vast majority of Chinese were peasants who owned a few acres of land, which they worked by hand. Good weather enabled peasants to grow enough food for their families and pay

their taxes. When drought or floods caused poor harvests, peasants would borrow crops or money from their leaders and the nobility. Many peasants would sell their land to pay off debts. Then, to support their families, peasants would work for the landowners as tenant farmers.

This was not a feudal system that forced the peasants to remain on the land forever. They were free to buy and sell land. In addition, peasants could take the government examination that would allow them to become officials. In practice, it was difficult for peasants to save enough money to buy land or pay a tutor to prepare them for the examination.

Mandate of Heaven

The earliest emperors claimed to rule by the Mandate of Heaven. A family could stay in power as long as its policies benefited the people. Heaven, a vague godlike power, judged the emperor's rule, however. And Heaven sent clear signs if dissatisfied with a ruler. Earthquakes, floods, famines, even comets and eclipses signaled that an emperor was failing.

In addition to natural tragedies, weak leadership preceded changes in dynasties. Corrupt emperors and officials sought more wealth and power. To obtain more money, government took over industries such as salt, iron, and tea. Taxes were raised to pay for expensive lifestyles of the emperor or his officials. Peasants would have to sell land to pay taxes.

These kinds of problems increased before each change in China's dynasties. Dissatisfied groups, especially peasants, rose up in protest. Usually, they looked to a special group in society to lead them: often men who passed the government exams but

A statue of Zhu Ge Liang, an advisor to Emperor Liu Bei

were unemployed or low-level officials, and sometimes merchants, fed up with high taxes. These revolts were a sign the emperor had lost the Mandate of Heaven.

The Glory That Was China

The first Qin emperor set up his capital in Xi'an in 221 B.C. It remained the capital, off and on, for 1,000 years. In 1974, while digging a well in a nearby village, peasants uncovered parts of the now famous Qin Pottery. These life-sized figures include nearly 7,500 uniformed warriors, each with distinct facial features. Hundreds of terra-cotta horses, thousands of clay weapons, and dozens of chariots were also found.

The city of Xi'an is famous in history as the starting point of the Silk Road. The Romans did not know the country's name, but they knew their expensive silk came from a faraway land. They called it the Land of Silk.

Marco Polo, the famous Venetian merchant, followed the Silk Road in the 13th century on his way to China. Eventually, he worked as a representative to parts of China for Emperor Khan Khubilai (Kublai Khan). He often sailed on one of the world's longest canals, the Grand Canal. The canal was built between the 6th and 13th centuries to link the Huanghe near Beijing with the Changjiang at the port city of Hangzhou, just south of Shanghai. It covers over 1,000 miles (1,610 kilometers), and sections of it are still in use.

Europeans and Arabs traded with China for its porcelain. It became so popular that Europeans started calling it china, as it is still called today. During the Tang (Táang) dynasty (A.D. 618–907), the white porcelain made in Jiangxi Province was so fine that people called it "artificial jade."

The Chinese also excelled in science and technology. The Chinese are credited with making the first compass, around the third century B.C. Another Chinese invention, around the eighth century A.D., was gunpowder. In China, it is still called "fire medicine."

Paper was in common use in China by A.D. 100–200. During the Tang dynasty, the Chinese carved manuscripts on blocks of wood. In 971, the first Song (Soòng) dynasty (960–1279) emperor had Buddhist scriptures printed. The printers used 130,000 blocks, and it took 12 years to complete the 5,048

Apartment buildings line the Grand Canal at Wuxi. ▶

volumes. The world's first movable type also appeared during this period.

Chinese medical knowledge goes back thousands of years. Acupuncture, applying small needles to points of the body to cure diseases, was practiced before 2500 B.C. Medicines used 2,000 years ago are still used in China for treating asthma, malaria, and other illnesses. By the Song dynasty, the Chinese had already published many detailed medical works on internal

medicine, surgery, orthopedics, and neurology.

In astronomy, no country surpassed the early Chinese. By 2600 B.C., they had calculated the solar year. They tracked comets, first recorded in 611 B.C., and described solar eclipses—the earliest one dated was February 22, 720 B.C.

Decline

Until the 18th century, Chinese science and technology was probably the most advanced in the world. However, a slow decline set in that would cut China off from the technological progress that was developing in Europe. Why did this great civilization fall behind Europe in science and technology?

One reason often given is ethnocentrism, a belief that one's own people are superior. The Chinese believed they could learn nothing new from the outside world.

Foreigners visiting China were expected to kowtow, or kneel in front of the emperor to show courtesy and recognition of China's superiority. Visitors also had to bring presents as tribute to the emperor. Of course, some foreigners simply considered this a part of the diplomacy to get trade.

The Chinese always looked on their trade with India, Africa, and Europe as diplomatic instead of economic. The goods that came into China were gifts to the emperor, not articles of trade. Confucian officials believed that the Chinese were superior to all foreigners and discouraged contact with them. Eventually, by the mid-1700s, the Manchu rulers had severely restricted contact with foreigners. Foreign representatives were not allowed to live in Beijing or travel freely in China.

Under Confucianism, the Chinese had built up a self-sufficient society. Whenever new ideas entered China, they were molded to fit Confucian teachings. At China's peak, in the early 1700s, the Qing (Chīng) emperors (1644–1912) continued to look to the past for guidance. China needed only to follow the rules of Confucius to have the good life.

Another obstacle to progress was the traditional Chinese attitude toward nature. Chinese philosophy, especially Daoism, teaches that humans must blend in with and accept nature, not try to master it. By contrast, the Western world was moving into an age of scientific analysis and attempting to understand and conquer the forces of nature. By closing itself off from the world, China slowed its progress in science and technology.

The Struggle for China

During the 1800s, powerful European nations forced the Qing rulers to "open up" to foreign trade. China tried to resist, but without the technology of the West, the Chinese were doomed to fail.

Their first major defeat came against the British in the Opium War, 1839–1842. By that time, opium had become Britain s most profitable item of export. As the British brought more and more to China, addiction among the Chinese was destroying families. Chinese merchants fought one another to buy the opium and then sell it to the people. Violence spread throughout the southern part of China. Seeing the destructive effect opium addiction was having on his people, the emperor tried to stop the opium trade, especially at the port of Guangzhou. But the British demanded the right of free trade.

The resulting war was short and disastrous for China.

The treaty's terms set the tone for other nations seeking special privileges in China. Countries could send officials to reside in Beijing for the first time. Foreigners with passports were allowed to travel freely in China. Hong Kong was given to Great Britain. And the opium trade was legalized.

By 1860, China had given up many rights of nationhood. Up and down the coast, ports were opened to free trade. Great Britain, France, Germany, Portugal, Russia, Japan, and the United States joined in dividing up China's port cities into their own trading centers. By the 20th century, China was close to losing its independence.

Signs suggested that Heaven had withdrawn its mandate from the Qing rulers to govern. Besides the defeat by foreigners ("barbarian devils"), famine and floods were unusually severe. And government corruption was widespread.

Reaction in China to these signs was abrupt and severe. One group sought reform by reviving Confucian tradition. Others looked to Western ideas.

Rebellion

Groups of Chinese tried to overthrow the Qing emperors. One rebellion was led by the Taiping (Tìe-Píng), a Chinese Christian group. In the 1850s, they received wide support by keeping strict personal discipline and helping the common people. After a decade of fighting, however, the leaders became corrupt. And the emperor's forces eventually defeated them.

As the 20th century approached, another rebellion spread rapidly across northern China. Unlike previous ones, leaders of this group supported the Qing rulers. Under the slogan "Support the Qing, destroy the foreign," the Boxers killed thousands of Chinese Christians and about 250 Westerners. Eleven Western nations sent 2,100 troops from the port of Tianjin to "liberate" foreigners in Beijing. While defeating the Boxers, the troops also managed to destroy many ancient landmarks in the capital.

The Qing remained in power, trying to reform by mixing Confucian values with Western technology and science. But by the first decade of the 20th century, the movement to overthrow not merely the Qing dynasty but the imperial system of China itself was gaining strength.

The 20th Century

In 1912, eight-year-old Pu Yi (Pǔ Yí) gave up his claim to rule China, and 2,000 years of imperial rule ended.

Three main forces came together to force this change.

One was the lack of authority in regional affairs by national officials. As a result, regional and village nobility controlled tax collection and work projects. They also raised their own armies to protect their power.

Another force that contributed to the overthrow of imperial rule was the rise of degree-holding men moving to the cities. Many got involved with commerce. Others worked hard to modernize China's industries. Still more found no jobs. And almost all of them spoke out for reform of the old system of government.

The third force was nationalism. The Chinese blamed many of the disasters in China during the 1800s on the "foreign" rule of the Manchus. Added to this was the increasing demand for some kind of constitutional government that would guarantee local self-government. Also important was the pride the Han Chinese had in their heritage.

In October 1911, local officials in Sichuan Province had negotiated for foreign money to build a railroad. The national government tried to take over the project, but the Sichuan officials rebelled and declared their independence from the Qing rulers. On January 1, 1912, they established the Chinese republic with its capital in Nanjing and Sun Yat-sen (Sun Yaht-sen) as its president.

The new republic faced two serious problems: (1) foreign nations occupied Chinese territory and (2) Chinese warlords (military leaders) controlled large areas of the country. In the struggle to solve these problems, three men towered above the rest: Sun Yat-sen, Mao Zedong, and Chiang Kai-shek (Jiang Jieshi—Gee-ăang Jyèah-shír).

Sun Yat-sen had studied in Hawaii and then received a medical degree in Hong Kong. But his passion was to reform China. In 1895, he and some friends plotted to overthrow the Qing rulers. Although the plot was discovered, Sun escaped. While living in Japan, he started a new revolutionary movement for a new China. In 1912, the group became the Guomindang (Gwáw-mín-dăng, GMD), or Nationalist Party, with Sun Yat-sen as leader.

Sun is best remembered as the spiritual leader of the new republic. He put forth his Three Principles of the People: democracy—the people should choose their leaders; livelihood—everyone should have food and work; and nationalism—all foreign privileges should be eliminated.

Modern Chinese Nationalism

Soon after the new republic was declared, China became a victim of the major powers fighting in World War I. Japan was expanding in the Far East and in 1915 demanded that China turn over more territory to Japan. This agreement, known as the Twenty-one Demands, would have put much of China under Japanese control.

Although it failed to get everything in the demands, Japan did keep Qingdao city and the Shandong Peninsula in the treaty ending World War I. In 1919, the Chinese protested, led by Beijing University students. The Chinese still commemorate this as the May Fourth Movement.

On May 4, 1919, 3,000 students demonstrated in Tiananmen Square against the Chinese officials who had agreed to the treaty. Violence broke out, and dozens of students were arrested. In June, merchants and workers joined in with strikes and boycotts.

The May Fourth Movement gave birth to new nationalist groups, most led by students and intellectuals. One group taking root at this time was the Chinese socialists, with Mao Zedong present at the early meetings. This evolved into the Chinese Communist Party, formed in 1921.

In 1925, Sun Yat-sen died and the burden of leadership shifted to the shoulders of Chiang Kai-shek. For a while, Chiang cooperated with the Communists in fighting against the warlords. But he never trusted the Communists. In May and June 1925, workers and students protested in Shanghai and Guang-zhou against foreign privileges. Strikes and boycotts followed.

In April 1927, Communist-led labor unions took over Shanghai. With support from foreign armies and Shanghai's underworld, Chiang's men attacked the workers and executed their leaders, marking the end of Communist-GMD cooperation.

Chiang's armies had defeated most of the warlords, so he turned to his next goal: defeating the small Communist army. His chances for success, however, evaporated when Japan invaded Manchuria in 1931. Chiang had two enemies to contend with now: the Japanese, beginning their march south into mainland China, and the Communists, who retreated from Chiang's attacks but set up their own governments in the countryside.

Mao was a master at combining theory and practice. He connected the harsh living conditions of Chinese peasants with the Marxist idea of class struggle. Instead of urban workers overthrowing the owners of industry, Mao substituted the peasants rising up against the landlords. To fight against Chiang's superior army, Mao used guerrilla warfare. His slogan: "The enemy advances, we retreat; the enemy halts, we harass; the enemy tires, we attack; the enemy retreats, we pursue."

The Long March

In October 1934, nearly 100,000 Communists began a retreat from Chiang's forces in southeastern China. Only a few thousand completed the 6,000-mile (9,670-kilometer) trek, which ended a year later in Yanan, Shaanxi Province. Tens of thousands died on the way, but the Long March has become a legend. Its survivors are revered as an elite group of heroes.

While Mao and his forces were camped in Yanan, he began his "thought-reform" program. People identified as having anti-Communist ideas had to write self-criticism, admitting their errors. Usually they were paraded before the public as political

A photo of Mao Zedong hangs in front ▶
of the Imperial Palace in Beijing.

enemies. In time, the guilty would discard their old thinking and be reborn into the community of the Communist Party. Thought reform remained a major form of party discipline until the late 1970s.

World War II and Communist Victory

To defeat Japan, the Communists and the GMD agreed to a cease-fire. By 1939, Japan's military occupied much of eastern China. But they never understood the power of Chinese nationalism. Factories, businesses, and government agencies packed up and fled to the interior. The Japanese could occupy the land, but they could not defeat the Chinese spirit.

The agreement between Chiang and Mao lasted only as

long as they had a common enemy. When Japan surrendered in 1945, at the end of World War II, Chiang and Mao resumed their struggle for control of China. Chiang's overconfidence led to his making many military mistakes. And in economics, he did little to stop inflation, high taxes, or profiteering. The signs from Heaven were not in his favor.

Communist troops followed strict military discipline. The soldiers, most of them peasants themselves, understood the common people. The Communists also took land from rich landowners and distributed it to the poor. In short, Mao won by appealing to the immediate needs of the common people.

On October 1, 1949, Mao led his successful forces into Beijing and announced the beginning of the People's Republic of China. Chiang retreated with hundreds of thousands of his supporters to the island of Taiwan. There Chiang set up an independent Chinese republic, hoping someday to regain the mainland. Today, Taiwan remains independent, and sentiment for reunification with mainland China is declining.

Soon Mao had controlled inflation, stopped all foreign privileges, rounded up criminals and prostitutes for reeducation, organized people for public works projects, and liberated women. Although poor, the people felt a new spirit of national pride under Mao's strong, dynamic leadership.

In the rural areas, Mao set up a system of communes. A commune consisted of 15 brigades, and a brigade was made up of 7 work teams, each with about 150 people. Crops belonged to the group, not the individual farmers. So the commune leaders decided how much the brigades kept. Brigade leaders then divided up that portion and distributed it to the work teams. Then the peasants got their share from the work team leaders.

Continuous Revolution

Mao wrote, "The true way that governs the world of men is that of radical change." He believed society would slip back into selfishness and greed. So the process of reform should never end; there must be continuous revolution.

At the top of Mao's hit list were landlords. Millions were attacked, taken before public trials, terrorized, and even executed. Any group connected with Western culture or capitalism could be targeted. Even teachers and artists were dragged from their offices and homes and humiliated in public. By the mid-1950s, China's economy still had not recovered from World War II and the civil war. Many party leaders wanted to use the expertise of non-Communist intellectuals who remained loyal to the government.

In 1956, Mao encouraged intellectuals to criticize the party leadership and policies. He announced the Hundred Flowers Campaign: "Let a hundred flowers bloom, let a hundred schools of thought contend." He was hoping for criticism that would reinforce Communist ideas and methods. But what he got was severe criticism of both the party leadership and of Communist theory itself.

Mao reacted by reemphasizing class struggle as the cornerstone of Communist rule. And he lashed out at the intellectuals, accusing them of being Rightist (enemies of the people). The Anti-Rightist Campaign began in June 1957 and lasted for two years. By some estimates, 800,000 people lost jobs because they were labeled Rightist.

At the same time, the Chinese suffered from a disastrous economic program called the Great Leap Forward. Mao wanted to step up production in agriculture and industry immediately. So peasants were put to work building flood control projects, while at the same time they were expected to increase crop production and build small industry in the rural areas.

Reports from all over the country claimed record harvests and industrial production. Unfortunately, the reports were false, covering up heavy failures. Peasants starved, disease spread, and the economy was almost destroyed. Between 1958 and 1960, 20 million to 30 million people died from malnutrition and famine. The Great Leap Forward nearly destroyed Mao's leadership. More than ever, he had to share his power with moderates—those who sought gradual rather than radical change—in the Communist Party.

Cultural Revolution

In the 1960s, Mao began another campaign against his rivals. He accused many party members of living like corrupt Confucian officials, with special privileges and comforts. In addition, he considered the younger generation a problem. Young Chinese had grown up lazy and had no feel for the life of struggle and self-sacrifice shared by Mao's generation. They must be injected with the spirit of rebellion to guard against slipping into individualism and capitalism. In 1966, Mao began the Cultural Revolution. The next ten-year period is often described as the "lost decade" by the Chinese today. Perhaps 60 percent of the party officials lost their jobs, including the man who would lead China in the 1980s, Deng Xiaoping. Even worse, as many as 20 million people may have lost their lives. Millions more were crippled mentally and physically.

School-age boys and girls joined a new youth group

called the Red Guards to "learn revolution by making revolution." Reciting slogans from a small red book, *Quotations from Chairman Mao*, they fanned out across the country to find enemies of Communism. They broke into homes, destroyed books, and beat old and young people alike. Some even turned on their own friends or family. China was edging toward civil war between the radicals and the moderates in the Communist Party.

In fact, the Cultural Revolution was a struggle within the party to see who would lead China in the future. The radical group behind the Cultural Revolution was led by a small group called the Gang of Four, which included Mao's wife, Jiang Qing (Gee-āang Chīng). The moderates wanted to end the chaos and destruction.

One moderate who managed to survive all of Mao's purges was Zhou En-lai (Chou En-lai—Joē En-Lái), who had accompanied Mao from the early days of the revolution in the 1920s. Zhou En-lai's reputation for honesty and loyalty became legendary among the people. Because of his remarkable qualities, he may have been the only man Mao could not remove from office. When Zhou died in 1976, hundreds of thousands of people gathered in Beijing to mourn. After Mao's death that same year, party moderates arrested and jailed the Gang of Four. Ever since, the moderates, led by Deng Xiaoping, who became the party's leaders in 1978, have run China.

The Cultural Revolution left a "lost generation" of idealists. Millions of people who might have been active in democratic reform became cynical about politics. No longer guided by Confucian or socialist values, they seem to be more interested in personal advancement than in political reform.

Opening the Door

China needed foreign aid to build up its industry. So Deng Xiaoping toured the United States in 1979, marking China's new "open door" policy. The door is now open to all Western technology and economic investment. What is unusual about Deng's policy, however, is his openness to capitalism.

"Our minds are on the left, but our pockets are on the right" is a popular saying in China. It suggests Deng's approach, often called "market socialism." To Deng, economic growth is more important than class struggle. He calls his system "Socialism with Chinese Characteristics." Perhaps Deng's pragmatic policies represent the genuine Chinese character more than Mao's ideas.

In agriculture, peasants can now lease land for themselves over long periods. They still owe part of their crop to the work team or village, but they can sell any surplus on the market for profit. Families are also free to pursue other kinds of businesses to make money.

Democracy Movement

Many Chinese want the door opened to political freedoms as well. For several months, from November 1978 to January 1980, Beijing citizens expressed their opinions with posters and poems on what became known as Democracy Wall. On this 200-yard brick wall, people called for open debates and democracy in China. Officials eventually tore down the materials and arrested scores of protesters.

Between December 1986 and January 1987, university students took the lead again in asking for change. In over 150

Tiananmen Square in Beijing. Mao Zedong's burial ▶
place can be seen in the background.

universities, students demonstrated for educational reform, against government corruption, and for more democracy. The government reacted by banning demonstrations.

Early in 1989, intellectuals in Beijing gathered to discuss democratic reforms. In April, a former government leader who had supported these reforms died. Thousands of students turned out to mourn his death. Emotions ran high as they marched with posters calling for democracy and reform. By May, hundreds of thousands were demonstrating in Tiananmen Square.

Students commemorated the seventieth anniversary of the May Fourth Movement with a peaceful demonstration. But this was the calm before the storm. In mid-May, students began hunger strikes. After meeting with students, government officials decided to call in troops. Refusing to give up, students erected a

30-foot-high (9-meter) sculpture of the Statue of Liberty, naming it Goddess of Democracy.

When troops entered the city, Beijing citizens joined students to block trucks and tanks. Then, on the night of June 3, the army moved through Beijing, firing into crowds. By the next day, thousands of civilians had been killed or injured. The government claimed over 1,000 casualties among the troops. Whatever the numbers, Chinese citizens were shocked that the People's Liberation Army (PLA) had crushed what was basically a peaceful movement by idealistic students.

The Future

The demands for democracy in China continue. But an underlying principle of democracy is that individualism takes priority over group loyalty. It is a principle that seems selfish to the Chinese, whose traditions stress the group.

The Chinese also distrust change from the outside. They take outside ideas (such as Communism) and mold them to fit acceptable Chinese philosophy.

Under their form of Communism, the Chinese have progressed rapidly. China is unified and free from foreign rule. Giant strides in women's equality and improved living conditions for the peasants have been accomplished. China has also become a major world economic power. The only question left is how to adapt political democracy to traditional Chinese theory.

4. Proverbs, Legends, and Literature

For more than 2,000 years, educated men have reached the top positions in Chinese society. The Chinese have always honored those skilled in language. As a result, the culture is rich in proverbs, legends, and stories.

Proverbs

Many popular proverbs are based on the word for eating—chi (Chīr). An example is the expression "We know how to eat bitterness." This combines the word for eating with the idea of enduring hard times.

Rice is so important to the Chinese that they use the word to mean "meal." When they invite people over for a meal, they say, "Come and eat rice." Another expression, "one bowl of rice," means "a good square meal" or "gravy train" in English. They also say, "The rice is cooked" to mean "What's done can't be reversed."

Animals appear constantly in Chinese proverbs. One of these is the fox. The fox "borrows the tiger's terror." This refers to people who bully others by showing off their powerful connections. But the fox "cannot hide its tail"—people will always give away their true character, especially if it's evil.

Here are some more sayings.

"Never burn incense when all is well, but clasp
    Buddha's feet when in distress." Do nothing until
    the last minute.

"Try to fish out the moon from the bottom of the sea."
    Strive for the impossible.

"Measure the sea with an oyster shell." Have a shallow
    understanding of a person or subject.

"Plug one's ears while stealing a bell." Deceive one-
    self.

"Dripping water wears through rock." Keep trying;
    little by little one will succeed.

"The gruel is meager and the monks are many." There
    is not enough food for everyone.

Tiger Legends

Another popular animal in Chinese culture is the tiger. During
the Song dynasty, according to one story, a priest rode around the
country on a special tiger on the fifth day of the fifth lunar
month. Everywhere he went, evil was burned to ashes, and de-
mons and monsters retreated underground.

In literature, tigers slay the wicked and protect the good.
Tigers are used as symbols for security and ideal marriages. In
Shaanxi Province, tiger figures are popular in dowries. Placed on
top of a lacquered chest, they escort the wedding party to the

beating of drums and gongs. "Son of the tiger" and "tiger's head" are two nicknames given to babies to suggest prosperity. Often children's toys and clothes are decorated with tigers.

Dragon Legends

Many popular legends in China tell about the mighty dragon, which symbolizes the powerful forces of heaven. In China's earliest days, Huang Di (Hwáang Dì—the "Yellow Emperor") went to the foot of Jingshan in Henan Province. There he mounted a dragon and flew up into heaven. He is called the Dragon King.

One legend tells of a terrible flood in central China 4,000 years ago. A man, Da Yu ("Yu the Great"), started upriver by boat to tame the river. But he was almost swallowed up by the deluge. A yellow dragon came and carried the boat up the river, and Yu was able to control the flood. He then founded the earliest Chinese kingdom, the Xia dynasty (2200–1750 B.C.). Ever since, the dragon has been the symbol of the emperors.

Dragons are also associated with the spring rains. On the second day of the second lunar month, the dragon raises its head, waking up from its winter sleep. The dragon growls and shakes its tail, making the sound of thunder, announcing the coming rain.

The Monkey King

Perhaps the most popular animal in Chinese legend is the Monkey King from the story *Journey to the West*. The actual events come from a journey made by a Buddhist monk in the 620s. In the story, the monk takes his disciples, Monkey,

Pigsy, and Sandy, across China to India to collect the Buddhist scriptures.

They have to overcome many obstacles. In one adventure, Monkey must get a palm-leaf fan to put out the fires of the Flaming Mountain, so they can cross to the West. Monkey tries to get it from Iron Fan Fairy by changing himself into a gnat and getting into the tea that she drinks. In her belly, he begins shouting and flies out of her mouth and onto the fan. He changes back to a monkey and leaves with the fan. But it's the wrong fan. She has tricked him because Monkey had been responsible for her son's death. Finally, Monkey has to go to the Ox Demon King at the Palm Leaf Cavern to fight for the fan.

Monkey and Ox Demon King each can change into 72 different forms. They have fantastic powers. They can sweep through time and space in a second. In one tremendous battle, both Ox Demon and Monkey become 10,000 feet tall and 8,000 feet wide.

Eventually, the Buddhist gods have to help Monkey, because he and Ox Demon keep fighting to a standoff. Monkey gets the palm fan and puts out the fire so they can pass. But before they do, Monkey discovers that the people living near the Flaming Mountain will continue to suffer drought unless the fires are put out permanently. Following the gods' advice, he waves the fan at the fiery mountain 49 times, and the flames go out forever.

Monkey used to live at the Jade Emperor's Palace (home of one of the high gods). But wanting to be free to live in his own life, Monkey kept playing tricks at the palace. Finally given his freedom, he challenged the Buddha, the highest god. He couldn't win, so he leaped thousands of miles to the end of heaven, only to find that he had progressed only as far as Buddha's hand.

As punishment, Monkey was sent to hell. When he arrived, he kicked over the furnace and some bricks fell to earth, causing the Flaming Mountain. So Monkey, in his desire to be free from authority, also was responsible for the damage. By escorting the holy man on the journey, Monkey is able to reverse this damage.

Although Monkey is called a king because he ruled over a kingdom of monkeys, he is a true hero in the eyes of the Chinese for challenging the corrupt leadership of his day. Ox Demon is like the feudal landlords with complete power over the common people. Throughout his journey with the monk, Monkey defeats evil forces, so he is a champion of the good. He refuses to accept defeat, even against the most powerful forces. Monkey fights on until he triumphs. Finally, Monkey is able to conquer nature, a force that has proven uncontrollable to the Chinese throughout history.

Today, Monkey's image appears on clothes and in television commercials. In addition, countless versions of the story exist in plays and movies. He is a true hero for the common people because he is also very human.

The Legend of Meng Jiang Nü

The husband of Meng Jiang Nü (Mùng Gee-āng Nŭ) was one of millions drafted to build the Great Wall. Meng Jiang Nü traveled a thousand miles to the coast east of Beijing to bring him some winter clothes. Upon arrival, she discovered he had died from the hard work. In grief, she cried so much that the skies turned black and it stormed. So much rain fell that the portion of the wall broke open and she saw her husband's bones. She blamed the emperor, but was afraid to challenge him directly.

The emperor wanted to marry Meng Jiang Nü. She agreed to the marriage if he would come to her dead husband's funeral and show respect. The emperor did as she wished. During the funeral, Meng Jiang Nü walked to the edge of a cliff, and with her husband's bones in hand, she leaped into the sea. There is a temple nearby, at Wangfushi Rock Village (Wàang-fōo-shír—"looking forward for her husband's return"). In the temple, there is a humanlike stone named *wangfushi* after Meng Jiang Nü. A famous ballad, "Weeping at the Great Wall," recounts this story.

Literature

China's tradition of excellent writing goes back at least 2,400 years to the five Confucian classics: *The Book of History, The Book of Songs, The Book of Rites, The Book of Changes*, and *The Spring and Autumn Annals*. Later famous books include *The Golden Lotus* and *Dream of the Red Chamber*.

The author of *The Golden Lotus* was Wang Xicheng. According to legend, he wrote the book to get revenge on the man who condemned his father to death. On each page of the book, which was made of rice paper, Wang put a drop of poison so that the pages would stick. He sent the book to the man, who read it eagerly. But to turn each page, he had to lick his finger. When he finished reading, he fell dead from the poison.

Many Chinese consider *Dream of the Red Chamber* their greatest novel. Hundreds of characters appear in the story, which was written in the 1700s, from maids and servants to mistresses and messengers. The story centers on the extended family of the house of Jia, the young hero, Baoyu, and the heroine, his distant cousin Daiyu ("Black Jade").

With their love of art and poetry, they become best friends. They disapprove of the "worldly" ambitions of the Jia family. Throughout the story, they come together in shy love for each other and then part after misunderstandings.

When Baoyu becomes sick, his family tells him he can marry Daiyu. But instead, his family chooses another bride, disguises her, and holds the wedding. Daiyu dies of a broken heart. After Baoyu has a son, he retires to a Buddhist monastery.

Although a memorable love story, *Dream of the Red Chamber* also exposes the corruption among the rich in 18th-century China. In addition, the novel reveals the power of the old Confucian rules that bound the young to their elders' decision. Even Baoyu, of such high stature, could not overcome his family's wishes.

Poetry

Poets have always been highly respected in China. In ancient days, nobles quoted from famous poetry in daily conversation. This was a well-established practice by the time Confucius began his teaching in the 6th century B.C. Confucius wrote, "If one does not study poetry, one cannot express oneself."

Today, students recite poems by scores of poets, but Li Bai (Lĕe Búy), who lived from A.D. 701 to 762, is perhaps still the most popular. His poems contain beautiful images and express deep emotion. One of his poems, "Seeing Meng Haoran Off to

Xingyin Pavilion, built in memory of poet Qu Yuan (340 B.C.-278 B.C.), who is called the "People's Poet"

Yangzhou from Yellow Crane Tower," presents his loneliness as he watches a friend sail away.

> At Yellow Crane Tower in the west
> My old friend says farewell;
> In the mist and flowers of spring
> He goes down to Yangzhou;
> Lonely sail, distant shadow,
> Vanish in blue emptiness;
> All I see is the great river
> Flowing into the far horizon.

The Future

Literature in the 20th century has suffered from the political turmoil in China. Under Mao Zedong's teachings, the role of literature is to reform society. Writers continue to publish, but they never know when their works will be censored.

Except for the most direct criticism of Communist leadership, the government has begun to show a more tolerant attitude toward writers. They frequently publish poetry and fiction critical of society and government. Young writers are starting to experiment with styles and forms of writing.

An "open" China refers primarily to economic growth. As long as the writers do not endanger that goal, they probably will continue expanding their range of subjects. Many of China's current writers have received praise throughout the world.

五

5. Family Life

Chinese parents spoil their children. The word for this is *ni'ai* (nèe-èye—"drown with love"). Until they are two or three years old, children usually sleep with their parents. Even in the daytime, children are rarely alone. Parents, grandparents, or daycare attendants are always around.

Chinese children are usually well behaved. Parents expect them to be quiet and obedient. Today, however, children are becoming more independent. Adults worry that these "little emperors" and "little empresses" value "vanity, comfort, and amusement more than hard work and frugality." Many people believe parents are spoiling their children today because each family is now supposed to have only one child.

One Child Per Family

Large families have always been the foundation that kept Chinese society steady. However, after centuries of encouraging large families, the Chinese realized they had to limit their population.

One way China's leaders try to slow the birthrate is to encourage people to wait until their mid-20s to marry. The government also gives out free birth control devices to married couples. In the 1980s, the government started the one child-one family policy. Parents who have more than one child are fined, sometimes as much as a year's salary.

The government's policy applies to the Han, but not to minority groups. They are usually encouraged to have as many children as they want. This leniency toward minorities illustrates the Communists' desire to allow minorities their own customs while maintaining loyalty to the central Chinese government.

Since living standards have improved, one out of every two Chinese is under 20 years old. Therefore, even following the one-child policy, the number of married couples wanting a baby will continue to increase for decades.

In the cities, the one-child policy is working well. Parents with only one child often receive a bonus from the government. The policy is harder to enforce in the countryside. Rural families often have several children illegally. Nevertheless, China is growing at a slower pace than most other nations.

Generation Gap

The one-child policy helps create a generation gap. Most parents were raised in hard times, when families often had very little, and everyone worked long hours. They don't want their children to suffer these hardships. But today's youth don't understand how difficult life was in the past.

More than ever before, families in cities have enough money to live comfortably. But instead of the parents, it is their children spending much of the money. The government estimates that primary and middle school students in cities such as Beijing spend half of their parents' income.

In the cities, young Chinese buy Swiss chocolates and other imported foods. They want to be seen in the latest fashions, in expensive leather jackets and designer jeans. They go to movies,

To slow population growth the Chinese government has instituted a policy of one child per family.

concerts, and video parlors. They have their own radios and bicycles. And all over China, they are listening to rock music instead of Chinese classical operas and folk music. Instead of China's classics, boys prefer "martial art" fiction, and girls read popular stories displaying emotions and romance.

Family Budget

An average salary for a city worker is about $40 a month. This figure is misleading, however. Usually, both husband and wife work full-time, doubling the monthly income to about $80. And almost all workers get bonuses in money and food.

The employers often pay workers' bus fares to and from work. And several times a year, the *danwei* gives workers rice, fruits, and vegetables. So, added together, these extras increase the monthly income of the individual worker to over $100.

The Chinese urban family pays very little for most other

necessities. The *danwei* provides apartments for free or only $1 or $2 a month and pays the family's medical expenses. Electricity and heat are free. And the family pays no taxes.

Food costs vary, but a city family of three can eat healthy meals each day for about $60 a month. Some typical prices for foods might be 8¢ for a pound of spinach, 60¢ for a pound of pork, 20¢ for a pound of fruit, and 10¢ for a pound of rice.

City and Country Living

Life in the cities is more comfortable than in the rural areas. For example, most city people in the north have radiator heat in the winter. However, most people living in rural areas have to buy coal or wood to heat their homes.

The government supplies electricity to city residents. But it is still common for several city families to share the same water source. In some apartment buildings, there might be one cooking area for three or four families. In the past, it was common for several families to share a toilet, although new apartments often have individual toilets. As for bathing, most workplaces provide bathhouses for their workers and families.

In cities, most families own basic household furniture such as sofas, beds, wardrobes, fans, and dining tables. Most families have one or two bicycles, a radio, and a television, and many have a cassette player.

Refrigerators are rarer, however. Only one in ten families in cities owns one. Because electric stoves are still too expensive, many people still cook on a two-burner coal stove. However, gas stoves are becoming more and more popular today.

In the countryside, most villages have electricity. But

Agricultural workers in the fields at Wuxi ▶

authorities often turn it off in the early evening to save money. Many students study at night by either kerosene lamp or a bare 40-watt lightbulb. Televisions are not as common as in cities. Only about one in ten families in the countryside owns a TV. However, most rural families have sewing machines, and almost every family has at least one bicycle.

Farmers have to pay taxes, officially about 5 percent of their income or crop. Often, however, other fees are required. Farmers might be charged fees for land rent, irrigation, electricity, aid for the elderly, and insurance.

In the country and cities, everyone shops at markets for food. More and more, these are "free markets," where prices are not controlled by the government. Some people do their shopping during the noon siesta. About noon, the Chinese take a break from their work to eat their lunch. They don't return until 2 P.M. Traditionally, this is time for resting, but many people play sports or exercise before returning to work.

All over China, a housing shortage exists. In the cities, the demand for an apartment is so high that some people wait as long as seven or eight years for a one-room apartment. In the meantime, they must live in dormitories with three or four roommates, with friends, or with relatives.

Chinese farmers do not own their own land. But as long as they pay rent to the village government, the land stays with the individual farmers. Farmers can grow extra crops and sell them at "free markets" for whatever price they can get. As a result, farmers' income has almost tripled in ten years. Most food bought by the people comes from these markets.

A major difference between urban and rural living is in health care. City hospitals are usually better staffed and supplied with modern medicines and equipment. In rural areas, people often depend on visiting doctors or village clinics.

Only about 14 percent of the people in China have full health coverage. Complete health care is offered only to government and factory workers. In the countryside, only a few have coverage. Recently, the government has begun planning health care programs for people in rural areas.

Even with limited health care, the Chinese are healthier than ever before in their history. Since 1949, the average life span for a Chinese has risen from 32 years to over 70 years.

Food

The Chinese are famous worldwide for their cooking. And they love to eat out. All varieties of restaurants can be found in cities and villages. Some serve expensive meat dinners costing a month's salary. Others offer inexpensive meals of rice or noodles and vegetables for a dollar or less.

In the cities, fast food has arrived. Beijing now has a Pizza Hut, a McDonald's, and scores of "fast-food" noodle restaurants. The McDonald's in Shanghai is the largest in the world, with 700 seats. It serves over 1,200 customers a day. Near Beijing's Tiananmen Square, a 510-seat Kentucky Fried Chicken restaurant sells more chickens each day than any other KFC in the world (1,300 a day in 1990). A three-piece white meat dinner for two, with soft drinks, costs about five dollars.

But KFC is no match for traditional Chinese cooking. The Chinese take very little and turn it into a feast. Some popular styles of cooking are named for the provinces where they originate: Sichuan, Guangdong, Shandong, and Jiangsu.

Eating is a major social activity in China. Banquets are especially luscious, with ten or more dishes of foods. Usually they begin with meat dishes topped off with mushrooms and vegetables and roasted peanuts. Eventually, a large fish sautéed in sauce is served. Then comes the rice and, at the end of the meal, the soup.

The daily diet of the average Chinese is less complicated. They eat a lot of vegetables such as cabbage, beans, carrots, bamboo shoots, green peppers, celery, carrots, and cucumbers. Rice is eaten at most meals, and noodles are popular, especially in the north. Some dishes might be cooked in hot peppers, Sichuan-style. Much of the food is cooked with herbs, ginger, onion, garlic, sesame oil, soy sauce, and vinegar.

A well-known northern dish is Beijing duck, and, along the coast, seafoods are eaten almost every day. The people of Guangdong Province are famous in China for eating almost everything. There is a saying in China that people in the south "will eat anything with four legs except the table and chairs."

A popular dish in most of China is *jiao-zi* (gĕe-ow dzuh), a dumpling with meat and vegetable stuffing. It is very easy to prepare. Here's a quick recipe for 50 of these dumplings.

Jiao-zi

Dumplings:
>   4 cups wheat flour
>   1 raw egg
>   3/4 cup water

Filling—Choose from the following:
>   1/4 pound ground pork, beef, chicken, or 5 or 6 medium shrimp (shelled, drained, and minced)
>   2 or 3 dried mushrooms, minced (soak in water for 15 minutes and drain before mincing)
>   3 or 4 bamboo shoots, minced
>   2 cups minced vegetables such as celery, cabbage, carrots, mild green pepper, or scallions
>   1 water chestnut, minced
>   1/2 tablespoon salt
>   1 slice ginger, about the size of a quarter, minced

Sauce:
>   2 or 3 tablespoons rice vinegar
>   2 or 3 tablespoons soy sauce
>   1 or 2 tablespoons sesame seed oil

Cooking oil:
    2 or 3 tablespoons vegetable oil

Prepare the jiao-zi:
    —Put the filling ingredients together in pan and stir-fry in vegetable oil.
    —Put wheat flour in a big bowl.
    —Place the raw egg in the middle of the flour and add water until the dough is fairly stiff.
    —Knead the dough until it is flexible.
    —Put dough on a lightly floured cutting board and roll the dough until it is shaped like a long sausage about the thickness of a quarter.
    —Cut the dough into about 50 equal pieces and then roll each piece into thin, 3-inch (7-cm) circles.
    —Put a teaspoon of filling into the center of each dough circle.
    —Press the edges of each single dumpling together and pinch the sides so no filling will get out.
    —Boil 25 dumplings in 10 cups of water for 10–20 seconds. Stir them to prevent sticking to the pan. Add 1/2 cup of cold water and bring them to a boil a second time for 10–20 seconds. Repeat this twice more, and the jiao-zi will be ready.
    —Follow the same procedure for the remaining jiao-zi.

Prepare the sauce:
    —Mix, vinegar, soy sauce, and sesame seed oil in a bowl.
    Place the dumplings on plates and you're ready to eat.
    Pick up one with your chopsticks, dip it in the sauce, and enjoy!

Bon Bon Chicken (From *The China Daily*)

Here's a Sichuan dish that is easy to prepare. Warning: It is hot; you can reduce the amount of peppercorn powder and garlic.

    1 chicken breast
    water
    4 or 5 green onions
    1 tablespoon sesame paste
    1 or 2 cloves garlic, crushed and minced
    2 teaspoons sugar
    2 teaspoons sesame seed oil
    2 tablespoons vinegar
    3 tablespoons soy sauce
    1 tablespoon vegetable oil
    1 teaspoon finely shredded gingerroot

Use as much peppercorn powder as your tongue can stand.

—Put chicken in saucepan. Add water until half the chicken is covered. Cover the pan and boil.

—Cook on medium heat for five minutes, turn over, and cook five more minutes, or until chicken is done. Take the chicken out and allow it to cool.

—Bone and cut the meat into 2 x 1/2 inch strips.

—Wash onions and keep only the white parts. Shred them finely and put with chicken on a serving dish.

—Mix the remaining ingredients in a bowl and pour over the chicken.

—Serve cold. This dish serves one. Sometimes people eat this with sliced and peeled cucumber and shredded carrots.

六

6. Education

China has more than 182 million students, 130 million of them in elementary school. About 70 percent of elementary school students go on to three years of junior middle school (junior high). The remaining, especially the children of peasants, drop out to work. China's goal is for everyone to complete at least nine years of education.

Morally Correct

Until the 20th century, education in China meant studying Confucian ethics. Rarely did a peasant child get an education. And Confucian schools were closed to girls. The studies stressed moral behavior, not science or math. They existed to train government leaders.

In the 20th century, the Chinese have tried to redirect education into more sciences and technology. But they still emphasize morally correct behavior. Prior to the 1949 victory, "morally correct" meant living according to Confucian principles. Since then, "morally correct" has meant good citizenship according to the teachings of Mao Zedong.

Generally, students are asked to follow a set of high standards. The "Rules of Conduct for Pupils" include love of the country, good study habits, physical exercise and extracurricular activities, physical labor, plain living, respect for teachers and classmates, concern for the public welfare, and honesty.

In the schools, patriotism comes before everything else. Students learn to love their country and its leadership. They are taught that only under the party's guidance can China remain unified and independent.

Children are taught that true socialist morality requires politeness, honesty, and modesty. They're encouraged to learn strict self-discipline in all areas of their lives. These principles are taught in special civics courses, as well as in history class. In fact, all teachers are responsible for monitoring students' behavior.

To promote service and loyalty to the nation, the Communist's created the Young Pioneers and the Communist Youth League. The Pioneers are elementary school children selected to be members of this special organization because of their

good behavior and grades. It is common to see groups of these blue-uniformed children doing good works for their communities. In the middle schools, this honor goes to those selected for the Communist Youth League. When these young people become adults, many of them are invited to become members of the Communist Party.

Elementary School

Elementary school lasts about 40 weeks a year for six years. Students usually have 12 weeks off for winter and summer vacations. Eleven subjects are taught in most schools. They include politics (which is basically training to be good citizens), Chinese, arithmetic, natural science, foreign language (if available), geography, history, physical education, music, fine arts, and manual labor. Students attend classes about 25 hours a week, six days a week.

Because of the difficulty of the Chinese written language, students spend about 40 percent of their class time on Chinese. They must learn 3,000 characters and the modern phonetic system of writing Chinese with roman letters, called Pinyin (Pǐn-yǐn).

To move up the educational ladder in China, students must score high on three entrance exams. Elementary school students must pass entrance exams to go to junior middle school, and junior middle school graduates must pass exams to enter senior middle school. The pressure to pass weighs heavily on students. They must memorize almost everything they study. And the best schools, called key schools, take only the top-scoring students. Key schools receive more government money,

◄ *A girl wears a Young Pioneer uniform at the YaLi Festival.*

Second-grade school children in Beijing

obtain more up-to-date supplies, and get better-trained teachers than the other schools.

Secondary School

Secondary schools are divided into two three-year levels, junior and senior middle school. About 46 percent of the graduates from junior middle school attend senior middle school. Most senior middle school graduates go out to work, but perhaps 33 percent continue some kind of college study.

About one-third of the middle school students attend schools specializing in vocational and technical fields. These schools offer intensive training in one of eight areas: agriculture, engineering, forestry, medicine, finance, politics and law, sports, and the arts. It is difficult to convince parents to send children to a vocational school if they qualify for an academic school.

The course load in middle school is heavy. Students attend about 30 classes in a six-day week, for 40 weeks. During all six years, students take political education, Chinese, math, foreign language (usually English), and physical education. Physics is taught in the last five years, and chemistry in the last four. Other regular courses include history, geography, biology, physiology and hygiene, music, and fine arts. Depending on the school, students may take several elective courses, ranging from computer science, astronomy, electronics, and oceanography to the theory of literature and art.

About 25 percent of senior middle school students take the national college entrance examinations every year. Of the more than two million students taking the exams, about one-third (600,000) will score high enough to enter college. Again, the pressure from parents and teachers to score high is very intense.

Held in July throughout the country, the exams last three days and determine who will be invited to enter colleges. All students are tested on politics, Chinese, mathematics, and foreign languages. The liberal arts students are also tested on history and geography; the science students take additional tests in physics, chemistry, and biology.

University

The elite of China's students attend college. China's government decides how many college graduates the nation needs in each subject. China has many specialized colleges such as those that train teachers, artists, musicians, dancers, and journalists. But a few stand out as the most influential. Beijing and Qinghua (Chīng-hwáh) Universities in Beijing are two of these.

Just as in their earlier schooling, college students stay together with their class for their four years of study. They live together in dormitories, usually eight in a small room (10 by 12 feet—3 by 3.5 meters). Typical rooms have two bunk beds on each side, and a table with a couple of chairs in the middle. Students keep their clothes and books in corners and under beds. Most universities have electricity, although the university may turn it off a few hours each week to save money.

All students on the same floor share a bathroom. But there are rarely showers in the dorm. Most universities provide a few communal showers in central locations for use by everyone on campus. Since hot water is limited to a few hours a day, it is rarely possible for students to shower every day.

Students wash their clothes using their own washbasins. To dry their wash, they often hang it on ropes stretched across the length of their dorm rooms. However, on sunny days, the dorm yards are full of laundry hanging on temporary lines.

The university provides dining halls for students, but they must bring their own bowls. The quality of food varies; however, in general it contains very little meat. It is mostly a gruel, a mixture of vegetables and rice. Students who have extra money usually buy special dishes of meat, or go off campus to buy better-prepared food.

On many campuses, students rise at 6:00 or 6:30 to the sound of patriotic music over campus loudspeakers. They are encouraged to exercise for 30 minutes before breakfast. Classes begin at 8 A.M. At midmorning, there is usually a half-hour break for more exercises. And then at lunchtime, the classes break for at least two hours of siesta. Many students take naps, while others play games such as volleyball, badminton, and Ping-Pong.

University students in a typical dormitory room

Then they return to classes until late afternoon. After dinner, most students go to their assigned homeroom to study for the next day's classes.

The life of Chinese students (at all levels) is hard compared with that of American students. Chinese students are watched carefully by their academic teachers, dorm supervisors, and political supervisors. Students who misbehave can expect a long meeting with any or all of their superiors.

Even for small offenses, students will lose face for being disciplined. And students might embarrass their friends as well as themselves. So peer pressure to follow the rules helps keep order and peace on campus.

University campuses are often like a small community. They usually have housing for faculty and staff as well as students. There are often stores with food and clothing, small market stalls selling fruits and vegetables, barbers, medical clinics, and many other services on campus.

The school year is ten months, divided into two semesters. The major vacation is for Spring Festival, which occurs at the beginning of the lunar New Year. This comes in late January or early February. Students also have a vacation during the summer, usually from mid-June to mid-August. Classes are held six days a week, with Saturday afternoon reserved for group meetings with their "political" leaders, who reinforce ideas of good citizenship. Unlike American students, Chinese university students take most of their courses in their major field. Besides their major, they are required to take regular classes in politics (Marxism-Leninism-Maoist thought).

Most students receive free tuition and room. They also get an allowance for food. But as expenses in China continue to rise, students find it hard to live on the allowance. Many get money from home or go out to work during vacations.

The government places most graduates in jobs related to their major field. Today, however, the government is allowing students more freedom to seek jobs on their own. Students who can find a business or agency that wants to hire them can get the government's permission to take the other job offer.

The Future

Slowly, Chinese government officials are trying to change the way students are taught. They have introduced learning as problem solving, with less emphasis on memory. They are also encouraging more enjoyable learning methods and adding more extracurricular activities. After school, students now participate in more sports, music, calligraphy, speech, and science clubs.

Educational reform will affect the exam system, which is already being revised. Soon students will have to take a middle school exam to receive their graduation certificate. Then if they want to continue on to college, they will take the college entrance exam separately.

The Chinese are trying to encourage science and math study. Throughout the country, there are now special schools called Mathematical Olympiad schools. Students attend these schools on Saturday afternoons and Sunday. They train students from the elementary level up for the national contests held each year. These schools are becoming popular. For example, the Beijing Mathematical Olympiad school has over 2,500 students coming for the weekend instruction.

The Communist government deserves high marks for raising the nation's literacy rate to about 75 percent. Now it is faced with an educated population in an era of immediate access to information from all around the world. The challenge for the government is to decide how to accept this great change while protecting Chinese traditions and cultural independence.

7. Festivals and Holidays

In every part of China, the people celebrate festivals throughout the year. Some are connected to the lunar calendar, such as the Spring Festival (the lunar New Year) and Lantern Festival. Others, like the Mid-Autumn Festival, deal with popular legends. Some, such as Qingming (Chīng-míng), a day for remembering deceased relatives, are connected to religious customs.

Spring Festival

China's most important festival, the Spring Festival, follows the lunar calendar and used to be called New Year. The lunar calendar follows the phases of the moon, so the lunar year is only 354 days. The lunar New Year falls on the second new moon after the winter solstice, sometime between January 21 and February 19.

This is the time for cleaning house, for beginning the new year with a fresh start. This is a five-day holiday in China. People dress up and visit friends. But it is a special time of year for families. Children and parents visit, sometimes the only time they see one another during the year. Children kowtow to their elders for gifts, especially money. Often these "little emperors" and "little empresses" get up to $100 to spend on themselves.

The most striking custom during this celebration is the bombardment of fireworks. For two days, the sound of fireworks thunders throughout the land without a break. This custom goes back thousands of years, to when the Chinese burned bamboo stems that expanded and burst open.

One legend tells of a mysterious beast with a human body named Nian (Née-en), who lived in a remote mountain. At the year's end, it would go into the towns and kill people and animals. Then people learned that Nian was afraid of noise and light. So one year they tried fireworks. The beast was so scared by the noise that it ran until its head fell off.

A famous Song dynasty poet, Wang Anshi, wrote in "The First Day of the Year":

> Amidst the sound of fire crackers a year is out.
> With spring breeze instilling warmth into the "tu su"
>   wine.
> As the morning sun shines over the gates of every
>   household,
> The old Door God pictures are sure to be replaced by
>   new peachwood charms.

Although people may no longer believe in the gods, they still hang the pictures along with New Year couplets. The pictures are believed to have begun in the Tang dynasty (A.D. 618–906). The emperor was sick and heard ghosts howling in his dream. Two of his loyal generals decided to stand guard outside the emperor's door each night. The dreams stopped.

The emperor thought it unfair that the generals had to stand guard every night. So he had images of the generals painted and hung the pictures at the entrance to the palace as "Door Gods." The custom spread quickly to the common people. Today, pictures are not just of the Door Gods. They include bouncing fish, a symbol of abundance; plump little boys; flowers; and birds.

During the Spring Festival, spring couplets are put on gates all over the country. They originally appeared in the Warring States period (403–221 B.C.) as charms written on peachwood plates. By the Song dynasty (A.D. 960–1279), paper was used. And in the Ming dynasty (1368–1644), one emperor passed a law requiring everyone to post two couplets on their gates. The custom is still popular today.

The Chinese are famous for their foods, and Spring Festival is a time for the best of delicacies. As noted earlier, the most popular food in much of China is *Jiao-zi*, the stuffed dumpling. In all of China, duck, fish, chicken, and beef are served. Also popular are sweets, especially *niangao* (née-en gāu), or New Year's cake. It literally means "sticky cake," but the words can also be understood to mean "soaring high every year."

During the fifteen days following the lunar New Year, lion dancing and drum and gong contests are popular. Other activities include stilt walking, dragon lantern shows, and stage shows with traditional legends such as Monkey King's adventures in *Journey to the West*.

Lantern Festival

On the fifteenth day after the lunar New Year, the first full moon of the year appears. The Chinese mark the day with the Lantern Festival. This celebration goes back to the Han dynasty (206 B.C.–A.D. 220). When Emperor Liu Ying died, Queen Lu took power. But she was not popular. When she died, the court officials managed to get the Liu family back onto the throne on the fifteenth day of the first lunar month. The Han empire thrived under the Liu family. On the anniversary of the family's return to

University students enjoy the elaborate lanterns at a Lantern Festival in Hebei Province.

power, the emperor would dress in common clothes and go out to mix with the people.

Displaying lanterns as part of the celebration goes back at least to the Zhou dynasty, more than 2,200 years ago. Common people were not allowed to go out or gather at night. But because this time of year was special in China's history, the emperor allowed the people to come out and celebrate during this period.

City and village streets on this night are as bright as day, with thousands of lanterns strung above the streets. They are designed and painted with a great variety of subjects, from pavilions and pagodas to landscapes and legends. Some lanterns are small enough to hold in the hand, while others are large enough to block out a large window.

Qingming (Clear and Bright Festival)

Over 2,000 years ago, a prince was forced to live in exile. Some followers went with him. But conditions were so hard that all but one returned home. One day, the prince wanted some meat, but there was none. So Jie Zitui, his loyal follower, sliced some flesh from his thigh and cooked it for the prince.

Later, the prince became the duke of Wen (Wún), head of the state. He decided to reward Jie by giving him a high title and land. Jie did not want wealth, so he and his mother withdrew to live a secluded life in the mountains. To get them to come out, Duke Wen set fire to the mountain, leaving one path for escape. But Jie and his mother wanted no rewards and stayed. As a result, they burned to death holding onto a willow tree. The duke had a pair of shoes made from the tree.

This event occurred on an ancient festival day called Qingming. To pay their respects for Jie's remarkable loyalty and modesty, people began putting out their cooking fires and eating cold food. In time, this became known as "The Day of Eating Things Cold."

By the Tang dynasty (A.D. 618–907), most Chinese were observing Qingming. In the early spring, they go to their ancestors' tombs to pay their respects. In the past, they would place food at the graves and burn paper money.

The Qingming festival also is a time to enjoy the spring. Throughout the country, young and old alike go outside to fly kites. The sky is filled with a great variety of shapes and colors, from legendary heroes to butterflies with flapping wings, and a wide assortment of animals. Although this festival pays respect to the dead, it is also a time to celebrate the coming of spring.

Mid-Autumn Festival

An important festival still celebrated in China is the Mid-Autumn Festival, originally held on the fifteenth day of the eighth lunar month. This night is supposed to have the brightest moon of the year, and full moons represent family togetherness. Another name for this festival is "Day of Reunion."

After a special dinner, families share moon cakes. Some of the big cakes, 1 foot (30 centimeters) in diameter, have carvings of the Moon Palace and Moon Rabbit. A famous poet in the Song dynasty, Su Dongpo, wrote: "A small piece of cake to eat as if crunching the moon; / Tasting like shortbread with maltose inside."

The most popular story told on this night is about Chang E (Cháang Uh). In one version, her husband, a cruel king, wanted to live forever. So he went to a magic mountain and found a medicine that would give eternal life. When he returned, Chang E stole the medicine and drank it herself. Soon she was swept up into the sky. To amuse herself, she thought to herself that she would like to visit the moon. Immediately she was at the Moon Palace and has been there ever since.

During the night, people go out to observe the bright moon. Tang poet Li Bai wrote a poem about Mid-Autumn that has become famous: "I raise my wine cup and ask the Moon to join me in a drink, / Facing my own shadow there are three of us now."

Learn from Lei Feng

To raise the people's awareness of the glory of working for others, in 1963 Mao declared March as "Learn from Lei Feng Month." Lei Feng (Láy Fūng) was a young soldier whose motto was "I am living in order to help others live better." He never did anything spectacular. He simply spent his time helping the common people around him. But his life was cut short by an automobile accident in 1962.

His unselfish character has been an inspiration for self-sacrifice among the people ever since Mao's 1963 campaign. Students perform good works during March every year. They help the elderly, plant trees, clean the streets, and do many other useful services for people and the country.

Schoolchildren recite this poem about Lei's self-sacrifice: "In the winter Lei Feng repairs cars regardless of the cold. / Lei Feng walks a thousand miles and does 10,000 good things. / Working for the Party and the people, his heart is red and never changes."

National Day (October 1)

National Day celebrates the victory of the Communists in 1949. Every year on October 1, local and national governments sponsor parades and sporting exhibitions. Bands play, the military marches, and fireworks fill the night air. Everyone gets a two-day holiday. Mostly, people relax with friends and family and play games.

Here are some important commemorative days observed in China.

January 1: New Year's Day. 1-day holiday.

January/February: Spring Festival. Lunar New Year, 5-day holiday.

February/March: Lantern Festival. 15 days after the Spring Festival.

March 8: International Working Women's Day. Women's holiday.

April: Qingming. Early Spring.

May 1: International Labor Day. 1-day holiday.

May 4: China Youth Day.

May/June: Dragon Boat Festival. At first, it honored the dragon, thought to be all-powerful. Later, it became a commemoration of poet Qu Yuan, who gave his life in 277 B.C. rather than submit to invaders of his homeland.

June 1: International Children's Day. 1-day holiday.

July 1: Founding of Chinese Communist Party.

August 1: People's Liberation Army Day.

September/October: Mid-Autumn Festival. Varies according to the lunar calendar.

October 1: National Day.

人

8. Art and Entertainment

On a sunny spring day, parks in China bustle with people of all ages. In one corner, couples tango and waltz to 1940s big band music. In another, a group practices traditional Chinese shadow-boxing (taijiquan—tìe-gée-chuán). A tape recorder blasts out the latest rock hit while young men compete at billiards. From a radio come the high-pitched voices of a Beijing opera. Beneath the shade of a ginkgo tree, singles and doubles smash Ping-Pong balls across gimpy-legged tables. High above them, dozens of multifaced kites dip and soar through the sky.

Near broad willow trees, mah-jongg (máh-geè-ang) players exchange the latest gossip while rapidly matching tiles like magicians. Some people exchange money at mah-jongg, although they could be in trouble for gambling if reported to local officials.

The edge of the busy street is lined with stalls selling stuffed animals and mechanical toys for children. And at one corner, two men sit beneath a tree, bent over boards, playing the ancient game of *weiqi* (wáy-chée), or "the surrounding game," better known in the West as "go." One player has 180 black stones (representing night), the other 180 white stones (representing day). They place stones on intersecting points across a board similar to a chess board. The 361 intersecting points represent the 360 degrees of latitude and the one "Basic Principle of the Universe."

The goal is to surround and capture the opponent's stones.

However, the game has much deeper meaning to the Chinese. Buddhists have used the game to discipline the mind. Go masters can look back on the record of a game and show exactly when a player became too greedy, tired, or careless.

On another street corner, people crowd around a fortune-teller. A few yards away, dozens are straining to watch a master calligrapher writing a poem. Along the streets, painters hang their scrolls, hoping for a sale. Vendors sell food, drinks, toys, souvenirs, clothes—almost anything imaginable. The streets are packed with people walking and bicycling. And everywhere there are children laughing and playing.

Tourists

For entertainment, the Chinese like to tour museums, zoos, and historical landmarks. Beijing is the most popular tourist spot. The city has dozens of museums, including the Military Museum, the Museum of the Chinese Revolution, and the Museum of Chinese History. Beijing also has one of the world's largest zoos.

Millions from all over the world visit the Palace Museum, in the Forbidden City, in Beijing every year. The Forbidden City, containing the Imperial Palaces, was the home of China's emperors from 1403 until the revolution of 1912. It was actually a small village within the city of Beijing, with over 9,000 buildings and palaces where the officials and all of their servants lived. The architecture is famous the world over.

Another popular city is Xi'an, an ancient capital of China, located in central China near the Huanghe. In southern China, Guilin provides tourists with spectacular scenery of misty

The pandas are one of the attractions at the Beijing Zoo.

hilltops along the Li River. Suzhou (Sōo Jōe) and Hangzhou abound with gardens and pavilions.

Tourists take the special boat trip along the Changjiang through famous river gorges. Thousands climb famous mountains such as Tai Shan, Huang Shan, Hua Shan, and Emei Shan, all sacred in China's religious past. In the summer, northerners flock to the ocean, especially to Beidahe (Băy-dàh-huh), south of the Great Wall.

In Guangdong Province, a new theme park is drawing tourists by the millions. Throughout the 74-acre Jinxiu Zhonghua ("Beautiful China") Park, the Chinese have recreated in miniature 74 of the most popular tourist attractions in the country, from the Great Wall and the Forbidden City to the 56-foot-high (17-meter) Buddha at Longmen Grottoes in central China.

About 62 miles (100 kilometers) northwest of Beijing, a

section of the Great Wall is open to tourists. From the spring through the fall seasons, thousands daily walk along this ancient symbol of China's independence. It is so popular the government uses the name to sell dozens of products, from Great Wall ties, suitcases, scarves, and T-shirts, to wine and jam.

Art

The Chinese spirit, however, still resides in its traditional painting. Developed from Chinese calligraphy, it is called ink-and-wash painting. This art covers three categories: portrait, landscape, and flower and bird. Using a soft brush, absorbent paper, and ink, the artist never changes the stroke once it is made. The function of color is mainly for contrast, never to make an exact likeness of objects. The goal is to capture the spirit and essence of the object.

Four elements blend together in this art: the picture, poetry, calligraphy, and the artist's seal. It is a magic combination of these that creates the overall spiritual effect of the best traditional Chinese art.

The Chinese are also famous for their decorative arts, their ceramics, lacquer, bronzes, and jades. The history of jade in China goes back 6,000 years, when it was considered sacred. Burial suits for powerful men and women were made from jade chips sewn together with gold threads. Jade represents good luck, beauty, and virtue.

After the Communists' victory in 1949, the Chinese went through a period of questioning their artistic past. The purpose of art, they said, was to promote good personal qualities and loyalty to the nation. As a result, creativity suffered for decades.

An artist at work on a painting in Beijing

During the Cultural Revolution, the Red Guards defaced many temples and statues across the land.

Today, the government is restoring these historical monuments. And artists are combining ideas from the West with their own classical training. They are returning to the spirit of traditional art, while expressing their own personal vision.

Movies

Like China's other creative arts, its movie industry has felt pressure to conform to Communist ideas. Many movies are produced by the government to glorify Communist military victories. In recent years, independent producers have been freer to express their own vision of society instead of repeating government propaganda.

Onlookers watch a movie being made ▶
at the Forbidden City, Beijing.

The best films and performers are nominated annually for China's Golden Rooster and Hundred Flowers Awards. The winners are usually movies popular in China, but not necessarily ones popular in the United States such as *The Last Emperor*.

In 1993, *Farewell, My Concubine*, directed by Chen Kaige (Chún Kăi-gūh), shared the top prize at the world-famous Cannes Film Festival in France. Another Chinese film, *Raise the Red Lantern*, was nominated in the United States for an Academy Award in 1992 for the best foreign film.

Red Lantern's director, Zhang Yimou (Zhāang Eè-mów), recently won international praise for his movie *Qiuju* (Chēeo-jóo)

Goes to Court. This movie depicts a woman fighting against corruption by going through the Chinese courts. It was named best film at the 49th Venice Film Festival, and the actress Gong Li won best actress for her part in the film. *Qiuju Goes to Court* was a big hit in China. Other recent popular movies include *Zhou Enlai*, a biography of his life, and *Smile in Candle Light*, about a middle school teacher. Each movie won several awards in China.

Some critics say the best Chinese movie produced since 1949 was *Yellow Earth*, released in 1985. A sad love story, the movie shows silent emotions rather than adventure and action. A Communist soldier has been fighting the Japanese in 1939. He goes to a small village on the Huanghe (Yellow River) to collect folk songs that will be used to build up Communist morale. The girl he falls in love with, however, has to marry another man picked by her family. Because the movie did not show Communists as superheroes, the government criticized it.

Many American movies, such as the *Rocky* series, draw huge crowds in China. Movies that show underdogs fighting successfully against corrupt, powerful forces are naturally popular in China. Other big hits in China were *On Golden Pond* and *Breakdance*. However, most imported movies come from Taiwan and Hong Kong because they share the same language and culture.

Television

China's first TV station opened in Beijing in May 1958. The government-owned station is called CCTV (China Central Television). Only state-approved programs run on TV, although the stations do run commercials for consumer products.

Today, 70 percent of the people have access to television. The most popular programs include game shows, sporting events, and movies. CCTV airs a nightly news program at 7 and 10. But half of CCTV's programs consist of educational shows and teaching programs.

Independent producers put out many good dramatic series in China. One of the most popular, "Expectations," is a 50-part series about a family raising an abandoned baby girl. Another award winner, "Four Generations Under One Roof," deals with the struggles of a large family in modern China. Foreign shows are also popular. Among the popular American shows on Chinese TV have been "Falcon Crest," "Vincent," "Remington Steele," and "Dynasty."

Traditional Music

A more traditional entertainment, especially in the rural areas, is the Chinese opera. Most large cities have their own opera troupes. Almost every night, a classical opera also can be viewed on television. The characters sing in high-pitched voices and move in a slow, artificial manner. They also wear makeup that represents personality traits. The plots come from classical Chinese literature. The young people of China sometimes don't appreciate the traditional Chinese opera.

String instruments have usually been used for folk, classical, and opera music. Two of these are normally played by women. They are the *gu zhen* (gǔ jūng), a little like a large steel guitar, and the *pi pa* (pé pa), similar to a mandolin with four strings. Another ancient instrument, played by men, is the two-string er hu (àr hóo). The player props the instrument

These actresses in the opera wear traditional makeup and costumes.

in his lap and strokes it with a bow. With these three instruments, the musicians are able to convey subtle but deep emotions.

Popular Music
The music of choice among the young is rock and folk. Current

singers from the West are favorites, but the most popular music stars are Chinese. The most popular rock singer probably is Cui Jian (Tswēe Gèe-an).

Cui's records sell out immediately. Among his best-known songs are "It's Not That I Don't Understand," "Have Nothing," and "Red Cloth." He sang "Red Cloth" to hunger strikers during the 1989 demonstrations in Beijing. The title song from his 1991 album *Jiejue* (Géea Jyéw—"Resolve") suggests the frustration of the young in China:

> There are many problems before us;
> There's no way to resolve them.
> But the fact that we have never had the chance
> Is an even greater problem.

Other stars on the rock scene include the groups Tang Dynasty, Panther, Yellow Race and Breath, Cobra, and Status. Their music ranges from the heavy-metal sounds of Tang Dynasty to the harmony of Panther. They all take defiant stances that make the government uncomfortable. In fact, Beijing officials wouldn't allow Cui Jian to perform onstage in the city.

Sports

The Chinese participate in a great variety of sports. Students from elementary school through college play table tennis between classes, during recess, and after school. Competitions range from the local to national level each year. Also popular are soccer, basketball, and track and field. And recently, baseball and American football have been introduced into China. Every

Members of an acrobatic troupe balance bowls during a performance.

year, American professional basketball games and the Super Bowl are aired on Chinese television.

In 1990, China hosted the Asian Games in Beijing. Nations from as far away as Kuwait traveled to China to compete. New stadiums and hotels were built in Beijing for the occasion. Chinese athletes won most of the medals.

In the 1992 Summer Olympics in Barcelona, Spain, China ranked fourth in total medals won: 16 gold, 22 silver, and 16 bronze. China's women swimmers won 4 gold and 5 silver. Chinese divers brought home 3 gold, 1 silver, and 1 bronze. In table tennis, a traditionally strong sport for China, the country won 3 gold and 2 silver. The women's team was especially strong, adding a silver medal in basketball, and gold in gymnastics, judo, and track and field.

Taijiquan (Tai chi)

Every morning, in rain, snow, or sunshine, Chinese—young and old alike—practice an ancient form of exercise called *taijiquan*. Begun in the 1600s, taijiquan consists of a series of circular movements that "resemble floating clouds and running water." The goal is to train people to coordinate breathing and exercise to control the body's movements.

It is one of many types of martial arts. All forms of martial arts are popular in China, from the leaping, "hard" school of the Shaolin (Shàu-lín) Monastery in central China to the slow exercise of *taijiquan*.

The Future

Although many of the elders think younger Chinese are throwing away their ancient traditions, this is not true. Mah-jongg, go, and other traditional pastimes still remain popular. Chinese of all ages retain deep reverence for their traditional culture. With painting and poetry as the cornerstones, the Chinese arts will continue to flourish.

九

9. Chinese Americans

The contributions of Chinese Americans to American culture are impressive. For example, the John F. Kennedy Library in Cambridge, Massachusetts, was designed by architect I. (Ieoh) M. (Ming) Pei. He came to the United States in 1935 from Guangzhou as a college student and became a citizen in 1954. He also designed the National Gallery's East Wing in Washington, D.C., and the John Hancock Tower in Boston.

In 1982, Americans dedicated the Vietnam Veterans Memorial wall in Washington, D.C. The wall was designed by Maya Lin, then a Chinese-American graduate student at Yale University. Four years later, she was asked to design the Civil Rights Memorial in Montgomery, Alabama. Today, she's an architect in New York City.

Why They Came

The first Chinese came to this country in the 1820s. Mainly peasants from southern China, many went to Hawaii to work on large plantations. Others were attracted by advertisements about the California Gold Rush in the late 1840s.

Once here, however, the Chinese found their opportunities restricted by language and racism. So they worked for low wages at any jobs they could find. Several thousands worked in the fields for private agricultural companies, especially in Hawaii and California. More than 20,000 helped build the first transcontinental railroad. Two thousand died laying track between California and Utah.

Discrimination

By 1852, one in ten—or some 25,000—Californians was Chinese. Almost all were men. White American workers, afraid of losing jobs to the Chinese, pushed their local and state governments to pass laws that kept Chinese out of many occupations. Eventually, California passed laws preventing any more Chinese from entering the state.

The Chinese were often harassed and killed. In 1871, 23 were killed in a riot in Los Angeles. An eyewitness reported, "Nearly all had been dragged through the streets at the end of a rope, and all were found shot and stabbed as well as hanged." In 1885, 28 Chinese coal miners were killed in Rock Springs, Wyoming.

In 1854, California's Supreme Court ruled that Chinese could not testify against whites in court. In 1871, the U.S. Supreme Court upheld a law that prevented immigrant Chinese ʌm becoming citizens. And in the 1880s, the U.S. Congress pass d its first Chinese Exclusion Act, intending to end Chinese immigration. Many states had laws preventing Chinese from marrying white or black Americans. Other laws in California prevented Chinese from owning land or sending their children to public schools.

A 1924 law prohibited Chinese women, even wives of U.S. citizens, from entering the United States. The law also stated that Americans would lose their citizenship if they married a Chinese.

As a result of this discrimination, the Chinese population in the United States dropped from 107,000 in 1882 to 70,000 by the 1920s. Only after World War II did the number of Chinese Americans begin to rise. In the 1950s, women were granted the same immigration rights as men. Congress then passed laws allowing close relatives from China to enter, resulting in more than 20,000 Chinese immigrants a year by the 1970s.

Chinese Americans playing Mah-Jongg at a festival in Dallas, Texas

Chinatowns

For their own protection, first- and second-generation Chinese Americans tended to stay together. As a result, over 96 percent of the ethnic Chinese in the United States live in large cities. They have crowded into sections of cities often called Chinatowns.

Historically, the Chinese are people who organize themselves into support groups. So it is no surprise that they have continued this practice in the United States. At both the national and local levels, the Organization of Chinese Americans (OCA) promotes equal rights and opportunities for ethnic Chinese. And in cities throughout the country, Chinese have formed neighborhood and work associations to both discipline and help one another.

In most cities, Chinese Americans have formed benevolent organizations. These groups assist in job placement, business loans, and even home building. In cities, ethnic Chinese often have their own Chamber of Commerce, cultural foundation, community development agency, and public safety association.

San Francisco's Chinatown, founded in 1858, is home to at least half of the city's 70,000 Chinese Americans. More than 200,000 ethnic Chinese live in southern California, with over 15,000 in Los Angeles's Chinatown alone. The largest Chinatown, however, is in New York City. Nobody knows exactly how many ethnic Chinese live there because thousands are probably illegal immigrants. But estimates range as high as 100,000.

Chinatowns are changing rapidly. Before 1950, most Chinese immigrants came from southern China. However, after the Communists' victory in China in 1949, the mainland was shut off. Thousands escaped to Taiwan and Hong Kong. From there, they often claimed refugee status and came to the United States.

Since 1975, ethnic Chinese who had lived for generations in Vietnam have fled to the United States. Many have settled in Chinatowns. San Francisco's Chinatown has about 4,000 Vietnamese. One Chinese-American leader there calls them "the new blood of Chinatown." In Los Angeles's Chinatown, Vietnamese own about half of the businesses.

Life for Chinese Americans is not always easy. Poverty is widespread, especially in the cities. Because of their traditional pride, many ethnic Chinese refuse welfare. The elderly often suffer from poor living conditions. In the 1970s, 86 percent of the Chinese-American families in New York City lived on less than $6,000 a year. Many were first-generation immigrants.

As they complete their education, second- and third-generation Chinese follow the American custom of moving to the suburbs. As a result, many small cities have large ethnic populations of middle-class Chinese. In southern California, they make up half of Monterey Park's 60,000 population. These are the success stories—the engineers, educators, and health professionals.

Success Stories

Numbering more than 1,500,000, Chinese Americans are the largest Asian group in the country. Nearly 70 percent are American-born. Their stories of success range across occupations: University of California at Berkeley's chancellor Chang-lin Tien; Nobel Prize winners in physics Chen Ning Yang, Tsung-dao Lee, and Samuel Chao Chung Ting; astronaut Taylor Wang;

Sun Cheng Hua (center) playing the Er Hu, a traditional Chinese instrument, with the Dallas Chinese Chamber Music Orchestra

popular Los Angeles city councilman Michael Woo; former Senator Hiram L. Fong of Hawaii; California Secretary of State March Kong Fong Eu; Monterey Park, California, Mayor Judy Chu; and Michael Cháng, a member of the U.S. Davis Cup tennis team.

They are excelling in the arts as well. For decades, classical music lovers have been enjoying the cello music of Yo-Yo Ma. Playwright David Henry Hwang won a Tony Award for his *M. Butterfly*. Bette Bao Lord has won national awards for her many novels. And both Maxine Hong Kingston and Amy Tan have won the National Book Award for their novels. Other novelists include Steven Lo and Gus Lee.

Chinese Americans work in every area of the movie industry. Millions of young Americans followed the movie career of Bruce Lee, the martial arts specialist. Tony Chan and Ang Lee are rising stars as directors. In 1993, Wayne Wang directed the movie version of Amy Tan's novel *The Joy Luck Club*. It became one of the most popular movies of the year.

Most Americans who watch TV network news have followed Connie Chung's career for over a decade. She is now coanchor for the "CBS Nightly News," a breakthrough not only for Chinese Americans but for women as well.

Perhaps Chinese Americans are making their greatest name in the sciences. Any recent list of national student science contests will contain several Chinese Americans. For example, the Westinghouse Science Talent Search gives out ten annual awards to top high school science students. The 1990 list had four Chinese Americans, including the second-place winner David Ruchien Liu, who won a $15,000 scholarship.

An Wang was born in Shanghai in 1920. He came to the United States in 1945 and earned a Ph.D. in physics from Harvard University. In 1951, he started a computer company, Wang Laboratories Inc., in Cambridge, Massachusetts. Until the microchip was invented in the 1970s, Wang's computers were extremely popular. By 1984, *Forbes* magazine estimated that he was worth about $1.6 billion.

Wallace Loh, born in 1945 in Chongqing, fled with his family to Peru in 1949. He was such a good student that he graduated from high school at 15. His family used their $200 savings to send him to college in the United States. Loh earned a B.A. in psychology, but no law school would accept him. So he finished an M.A. at Cornell and a Ph.D. in social psychology at the University of Michigan. Finally, in 1971, he was accepted by Yale Law School.

Loh taught law at the University of Washington and served as associate dean of the law school. He was voted best teacher in 1989. In 1990, he became the first Asian American to become dean of a law school in the United States. He credits his success with his "faith in the American dream that everything is possible."

Elaine Chao was born in Taiwan and came to the United States when she was eight. She graduated from college in 1975 and finished an M.B.A. at Harvard. Later, she worked on President Ronald Reagan's policy staff, and served as vice president at BankAmerica in San Francisco and as head of the Federal Maritime Commission. Under President George Bush, she served as deputy secretary of transportation. Then, in 1991, she was appointed director of the Peace Corps. Recently, she became president of United Way.

Going Home Again

Taishan County in Guangdong Province, southeastern China, calls itself "home of the overseas Chinese." Its 960,000 residents claim about 1.2 million relatives living outside of China. Money sent by relatives has funded 500 schools and 50 hospitals in Taishan County since 1982.

One of Taishan's natives has returned to his homeland to "do something for China—and myself." In 1949, 15-year-old Tommy Quan and his family left China and settled in Seattle, Washington. Over the years, Quan became a multimillionaire, owning restaurants, a ski resort, and real estate. He married and raised four children. Then in 1982, Quan decided to return to China to start a 300-acre orange farm. He wanted to show the people there how to become prosperous farmers. Today, he is known by the nickname Orange King of Taishan County.

Problems and Prospects

Chinese Americans whose families have lived in the United States for several generations maintain strong ties to their rich culture. They celebrate the Chinese New Year with parades and banquets. They also retain their heritage of strong family unity.

Even with their common heritage, though, the Chinese come from different social and political backgrounds. As a result, they form minorities within the Chinese community itself.

Since the mid-1980s, affluent Chinese have been coming from Hong Kong, afraid that when the mainland takes over, they will lose their freedoms. Little interested in politics, they often look down on mainland Chinese as being too political. The ethnic Chinese from Vietnam form a separate minority because the Vietnamese consider China their historical enemy.

Hundreds enter the United States each year as illegal immigrants. They borrow $30,000 or more to pay smugglers to get them out of China. Once here, they can only work illegally, so they accept jobs sewing in "sweatshops" or cooking and busing in restaurants. For six days a week, 10 to 12 hours a day, they labor for a dollar or two an hour in unsafe and unhealthy conditions. Often they are little more than slaves to the crime gangs that have smuggled them to the United States.

The Future

The majority of Chinese settling in the United States simply want to be accepted as Americans. A Chinese-American leader in San Francisco, Gordon Chin, said, "We hope to enjoy all the benefits of mainstream America while maintaining our cultural identity and integrity." That is the American dream, to be

Young girls perform a traditional dance during a ▶
Chinese New Year celebration in Dallas.

a member of the community, and at the same time keep one's individuality.

One out of six ethnic Chinese still works in a restaurant, but that pattern is beginning to change. They are now entering all areas of American life. Men and women Chinese Americans have graduated from the military academies, been elected to serve as city mayors from California to the Mississippi Delta, served as sheriffs of large cities, and piloted planes in combat. They are journalists, school counselors, lawyers, dancers, actors, surgeons, presidents of colleges, and TV news commentators.

Chinese Americans preserve their heritage of working hard and helping one another. In communities throughout the United States, they are making the American dream come true.

Appendix One: The Chinese Language

As early as 1400 B.C., the Chinese were carving picture messages on bones. These early characters developed into one of the world's first writing systems.

Picture a Word: Writing

For the *sun,* the Chinese drew a circle and a dot, ⊙. An *ox* or *cow* was a drawing of a head with horns, 𐀁. The *moon* was simply a quarter-moon, 𐀂. A *mountain* had three peaks, ▲▲. A *person* was shown by someone walking, 𐀃. Over the centuries, most characters have changed. For example, *sun* is now 日; *ox* (*cow*) is 牛; *moon* is 月; *mountain* is 山; and *person* is 人.

Characters are usually combined for their meanings. The idea of *good* uses *woman* on the left and *child* on the right, 好. *East* combines the sun rising behind a tree, 日 and 木 = 東, today simplified to 东. *Sit* places two people sitting on the earth or ground, 坐. The word for *see* has an eye on top of a pair of legs, 見, today simplified to 见.

Beijing, 北京, is *north* and *capital.* China's capital for hundreds of years, it's located in northern China. Nanjing, 南京, in the south, has sometimes served as China's capital, and it combines *south* and *capital.* Zhonggua, 中国, the word for *China,* is a combination of the characters for *center* on the right and *nation* on the left, or *middle kingdom.*

The most common way of forming Chinese words is by combining a sound character with a meaning character. An example of this is one of the words for *river,* 江, made up of the character meaning *water* on the left and the sound *jīang*. Another common example is a word for *visit, făng* (fŭng), 访; the left side is the character for *speech*, while the right is the sound for *făng*.

Spoken Chinese

Since the Qing dynasty (1644–1912), the Chinese have used *pŭtônghuà* (pŭ-tōng hwàh) or Mandarin, the common speech of Beijing, as their official language. However, different dialects exist throughout the country. Sometimes a dialect cannot be understood outside the native area. Mandarin, however, is taught in the schools and used in radio, television, and movies.

Chinese is complicated because a syllable can have four different tones (lines show direction of tone when spoken): (1) high and steady—*mā*, mother; (2) rising—*má*, hemp; (3) dipping and rising—*mă*, horse; (4) dropping—*mà*, scold.

At times, the same word with the same tone might have more than one meaning. For example, a popular dictionary lists seven meanings for the expression *tíng*, from "pavilion" and "front courtyard," to "stop" and "thunderbolt." There are over nine possible meanings for *hàn*, including "sweat," "drought," "brave," "chin," "regret," and "vast."

Add to this the various dialects that abound in China, from town to town and region to region. A dialect spoken in Guangzhou, in southern China, has nine tones, instead of four. It is impossible for someone not trained in the dialect to understand the Guangzhou dialect. Just an hour or so south of Guangzhou is Taishan, an area with its own dialect, which Guangzhou residents may not understand. Nearby, the people of Macao and Hong Kong have their own dialects.

Common Expressions

English and Chinese use mostly the same sounds. Some of the more difficult sounds in Chinese are **Zh** - j, **Z** - dz, **C** - ts, **Q** = ch, and **X** = between sh and sy. Final **a** = ah, **e** = uh, **en** = un, and **uo** = aw or ah.

Nǐ hǎo (Něe hǒw). Hello. (Can be used for morning, afternoon, evening).

Hǎo, xiè-xiè nǐ (Hǒw, syèah-syèah ně). Fine, thank you.

Zài-jiàn (Dzài jiàn). Good-bye.

Shì (Shìr). Yes.

Bú-shì (Bóo-shìr). No.

Duì-bu-qǐ (Dwày-boo-chěe). Excuse me; pardon me.

Méi-yǒu gūan-xi (Méi yǒ gwāan-syee). Don't mention it.

Qǐng shuō Yīng-wén (Chǐng shwaw-Yīng-wún). Please speak English.

Wǒ dǒng (Wǒw doǒng). I understand.

Wǒ bù dǒng (Wǎw bòo doǒng). I don't understand.

Qǐng zài shuō yi-biàn (Chǐng dzài shwāw ee-bee-èn). Please say it again.

Wǒ shì . . . (Wǎw shìr . . .). My name is . . .

Wǒ shì Měi-guó rén (Wǎw shìr Mǎy-gwáw wrén). I'm an American. (*Měi-guó* means "beautiful country.")

Qǐng bāng-zhù wǒ (Chǐng baāng-jòo wǎw). Please help me.

Wǒ yào zhèi-ge (Wǎw yàu jày-guh). I want this one.

Duō-shǎo qián (Dwāw-shǎu cheé-en)? How much [money]?

Děng-yi děng (Dǔng-ee-dǔng). Wait a moment.

Cè-suǒ zài nǎr (Tsù-swǎh dzài nǎr)? Where's the bathroom?

Appendix Two:
Chinese Embassies and Consulates in the United States and Canada

Chinese embassies and consulates want to help Americans and Canadians better understand the People's Republic of China. For more information about China, contact the consulate or embassy nearest you.

In the United States

Washington, D.C.
Embassy of the People's Republic of China
2300 Connecticut Avenue N.W.
Washington, D.C. 20008

Chicago, Illinois
Consulate General of the People's Republic of China
104 South Michigan Avenue
Suite 820, 900
Chicago, Illinois 60603

Houston, Texas
Consulate General of the People's Republic of China
3417 Montrose
Houston, Texas 77006

Los Angeles, California
Consulate General of the People's Republic of China
501 Chatto Place
Los Angeles, California 90020

New York, New York
Consulate General of the People's Republic of China
520 12th Avenue
New York, New York, 10036

In Canada

The Embassy of the People's Republic of China
515 Saint Patrick Street
Ottawa, Ontario
Canada K1N 5H3

The Consulate General of the People's Republic of China
240 Saint George Street
Toronto, Ontario
Canada N5R 2P4

The Consulate General of the People's Republic of China
3380 Glenville St.
Vancouver, BC
Canada V6H 3K3

A Time Line of Major Events in Chinese History

B.C.
(dates earlier than Warring States period are estimates)

Before 2500   Settled agricultural communities existed near the present-day city of Xi'an near the Huanghe at least 2,000 years prior to the Xia dynasty. Communities making pottery, growing rice, producing silk, and governing themselves as a village unit existed in other areas of China as well.

2200   Xia dynasty begins (Chinese)—Shang and Zhou states also exists, but Xia is the most powerful at this time.

1750   Shang dynasty begins (Chinese)—system of writing exists; style of architecture begins that is still used today.

1040   Western Zhou empire begins (Chinese)—often considered the earliest unified Chinese state; many of China's customs are traced to the Zhou empire.

771   Eastern Zhou empire begins (same family as Western Zhou).

551   Birth of Confucius.

403   Warring States period (7 major states fighting for control, although Zhou remains strong).

256   Eastern Zhou empire ends—short period of civil war.

221   Qin (Ch'in) dynasty begins (China gets its name from this dynasty). Emperor starts project to link together a series of walls, eventually becoming the Great Wall of China; writing is standardized.

206   Han dynasty begins (Chinese)—Confucianism becomes the guide for living and governing. China moves into modern-day North Vietnam and North Korea.

A.D.

100   Buddhism reaches China.

220   Han dynasty ends—330–400 years of rivalry between states begins.

265   Three Kingdoms begins, but rivalry and unrest continue.

317   Six Dynasties begins in southern China (Chinese)—civil unrest continues.

589   Six Dynasties ends—short period of civil unrest follows.

618   Tang dynasty begins (Chinese)—unity and internal peace give rise to a long period of great inventions, art, literature. China expands again into present-day Vietnam and Korea.

907   End of Tang dynasty—period of civil unrest follows.

960   Northern Song dynasty begins (Chinese)—many consider the Song era the peak of Chinese civilization.

1127	Southern Song dynasty begins (Chinese).
1279	Yuan begins 89 years of rule (non-Chinese—Mongolian). Khan Khubilai builds his capital at what is today Beijing.
1368	Ming dynasty begins 276 years of rule (Chinese)—finishes the Great Wall.
1644	Qing dynasty begins 268 years of rule (non-Chinese—Manchurian).
1800	China has fallen behind the Europeans in technology, and in the 1840s Europe forces China to open up ports for trade.
1912	Qing dynasty ends—China becomes a republic—followed by war against powerful regional warlords and then between the Communists and Nationalists (Guomindang).
1931	Japan invades Manchuria; by 1938, Japan occupies Beijing and the land past the Huanghe, including Shanghai.
1949	Communist government begins.
1978	China begins economic reforms.

Glossary

Buddhism—Buddhism is a religion that originated in northern India (present-day Nepal) with the teachings of Siddhartha Gautama (6th century B.C.). He taught that the reason for suffering in life was that people were too attached to worldly things. They put their trust for happiness in false hopes. Truth existed only in what was eternal, not in temporary material objects and relationships. There are several branches of Buddhism, but the popular one in China was the Great Vehicle, which is the more liberal and appeals more to the common people. Enlightenment, or salvation, goes to those who are able to realize that truth resides not in this world, but in realizing that they are a part of the eternal energy or soul.

capitalism—Basically an economic system that calls for individual ownership of property and businesses. Prices depend on competition and demand for products. China is rapidly spreading the system of free enterprise throughout the country.

Communism—A term originally used to describe the ideas of Karl Marx and Friedrich Engels. The first Communist leader of the former U.S.S.R., Vladimir Lenin, revised it. Mao Zedong took the general concept of Communism and reshaped it to conform to China's needs. Basically it is an economic term that means total equality in work and wages. But this stage of economic life can only be reached after society undergoes a series of changes from capitalism to socialism. Most Communists believed that these changes must be forced by the common workers/peasants by violent means.

Communist Youth League—One of the organizations formed by the Communist Party to encourage young people to learn about the party and to become loyal Communists. They also do a lot of community work and participate in parades, etc.

Confucius—Kong Fuzi, whose basic ideas are described in chapter 2, was the most influential person in Chinese history up to the mid-20th century. He was a teacher who wanted to become an advisor to a state official to help form the ideal state. He never found the position, but his teachings survived and had become the central core of Chinese culture by the 1st century A.D.

Cultural Revolution—From 1966 until 1976, China suffered greatly from Mao Zedong's attempt to discipline the people to become purer in their self-sacrifice and practice of Communism. Mostly, millions of young people were released from schools and encouraged to go around the country to preach to the common people and purge those whose behavior and past life showed signs of sympathy for capitalism and intellectualism. Only after Mao died did the government officials put an end to the decade of chaos. Today, the Chinese write bitter stories and criticisms of the period.

danwei—*Danwei* refers to a person's workplace—factory, school, or business.

Daoism—This philosophy/religion is associated with Lao Zi, described in chapter 2, who lived probably about the same time as Confucius. Essentially, it is a nature religion, based on the principle that humans should follow lessons of their environment, acting naturally rather than trying to overwhelm and control one another.

democracy movement—Although pure democracy probably doesn't exist anywhere, many Chinese today want to extend the participation in government to the people by devising a system that ensures a broad representation of the people in the government. In the late 1970s, spokespersons from different occupations, but especially university students and professors, began criticizing the failure of China's government to move toward a freer political system. In 1989, students across the country demonstrated against government corruption and sought a more active role in the government. This ended when armed Chinese troops were sent to Beijing to stop the demonstrations.

dynasty—*Dynasty* is simply a word used to describe the rule of a single family over the years, and in China, usually they ruled for centuries.

ethnocentrism—*Ethnocentrism* refers to the belief by an ethnic or racial group that their particular group is superior to all others.

free market—In both rural and urban areas, the Chinese have set up markets where people can sell their products for whatever price the competition will allow. Bargaining between customer and seller is normal.

Guomindang—The Nationalist Party set up by Sun Yat-sen, Chiang Kai-shek, and others in the early 20th century to push for the overthrow of the imperial system in China. The party emerged as the primary rival of the Communist Party for the heart of China after the late 1920s. After defeat in 1949, the Guomindang moved to Taiwan, where it has ruled since.

lunar month—According to the appearance of the new moon, each month is 29 or 30 days long. Ancient societies throughout the world measured time by the cycles of the moon and sun in order to determine when to plant crops.

Mandate of Heaven—As described in chapter 3, the Mandate of Heaven was a theory devised by ruling families to justify their taking and maintaining rule over the country.

minority groups—Ninety-four percent of the Chinese trace their ancestors to the Han people. But China's borderlands are dominated by different ethnic groups such as the Zhuang (southeastern China), Mongol (Inner Mongolia), the Manchu (Manchuria), and the Tibetan (Tibet). There are officially 55 ethnic minority groups in China.

moderate (politics)—A difficult concept to describe, but those officials who try to balance the extremes in China are considered moderates. Zhou En-lai is an excellent example of this. At times, Deng Xiaoping has leaned toward this position. Moderates might be called the more pragmatic of the Chinese politicians.

nationalism—Probably the major influence in 20th-century world politics, nationalism is the desire of a people to form their own country, to govern it without outside influence, and to be recognized as independent by the rest of the world.

opening the door—Throughout history, the Chinese have rejected foreign influences because they believed all non-Chinese were less civilized than the Chinese. Now, they are opening the door to foreign ideas because they realize that to improve the living conditions of the Chinese people, they must accept foreign ideas.

Pinyin—This is the current popular method for writing Chinese with roman letters. It means spelling according to the sound of the words (phonetic spelling).

radical (politics)—The *radicals*, in Chinese politics, usually refers to the extreme loyalists to pure Communism. They have been represented by those who supported the Cultural Revolution and, in much of his career, by Mao Zedong.

Rightist (politics)—Under Communist rule, a Rightist is anyone opposed to those in power. Usually, the term has referred to those in China who are associated with businesses, the West, and intellectuals.

socialism—As used by the Chinese, socialism is more than just state control of business. It also has included the social philosophy of unselfishly helping society.

warlord—In the early 20th century, there were powerful officials throughout China who controlled a large area, perhaps as much as a whole province. These men used the military to keep themselves in power. The warlords were opposed by those leaders, such as Chiang Kai-shek and Mao Zedong, who wanted a strong, unified China.

Young Pioneers—An organization that brings young students together into a group that encourages study of Communism, loyalty to the country, and good works for society.

Selected Bibliography

Aria, Barbara, and Russell Eng Gon. *The Spirit of the Chinese Character: Gifts from the Heart.* San Francisco: Chronicle Books, 1992.

Beijing Review.* Magazine.

Bodde, Derk.*China's Gift to the West.* Asiatic Studies in American Education, no. 1. Washington, D.C.: American Council on Education, 1942.

————. *Chinese Ideas in the West.* Asiatic Studies in American Education, no. 3. Washington, D.C.: American Council on Education, 1942.

China Pictorial.* Magazine.

China: 7,000 Years of Discovery: China's Ancient Technology.* China Science and Technology Museum and China Reconstructs. Beijing, China: China Reconstructs, 1983.

Ferroa, Peggy. *China: Cultures of the World.* New York: Marshall Cavendish, 1991.

Kitano, Harry H. L., and Roger Daniels. *Asian Americans: Emerging Minorities.* Englewood Cliffs, N.J.: Prentice-Hall, 1988.

LiXiao Ming. *The Mending of the Sky and Other Chinese Myths.* Durham, N.H.: Oyster River Press, 1989.

Luo Zewen, et al. *The Great Wall.* New York: McGraw-Hill, 1981.

Montanaro, John. *Chinese/English Phrase Book for Travellers.* New York: John Wiley & Sons, n.d.

*These and many other excellent books and magazines on Chinese culture and history can be ordered from China Books at:

2929 24th Street, San Francisco, CA 94110 (415) 282-2994

55 E. Washington, Suite 1003, Chicago, IL 60602 (312) 782-6004

They have excellent catalogues.

Another good source of materials about China and other multicultural books is:

Pem Press Division, Pathway Book Service, Lower Village, Gilsum, NH 03448 (800) 345-6665.

Index

About the Author

Tony Zurlo lives in Fort Worth, Texas, where he teaches English, non-Western literature, and ESL at Tarrant County Junior College—South Campus. His experience living and working in non-Western cultures is extensive, including teaching in Nigeria for two years with the Peace Corps and one year at Hebei Teachers' University in Shijiazhuang, P.R. China.

Tony has published fiction, poetry, essays, and book reviews for over a decade. He is also the author of the book *Japan: Discovering Our Heritage*, 1991, for Dillon Press. Tony's collection of poems about China, *The Mind Dancing*, is due to be published soon.